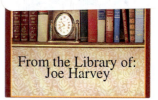

THE NAMES OF
JESUS

THE NAMES OF JESUS

An In-Depth Exploration of the Christ

RUBEL SHELLY

HOWARD
PUBLISHING CO.

Our purpose at Howard Publishing is to:
* *Increase faith* in the hearts of growing Christians
* *Inspire holiness* in the lives of believers
* *Instill hope* in the hearts of struggling people
  everywhere

Because He's coming again!

The Names of Jesus ©1999 by Rubel Shelly
All rights reserved. Printed in the United States of America
Published by Howard Publishing Co., Inc.,
3117 North 7th Street, West Monroe, Louisiana 71291-2227

99 00 01 02 03 04 05 06 07 08   10 9 8 7 6 5 4 3 2 1

Library of Congress Cataloging-in-Publication Data
Shelly, Rubel.
    The names of Jesus : an in-depth exploration of the Christ / Rubel
Shelly.
        p.   cm.
    Includes bibliographical references.
    ISBN 1-58229-058-X
    1. Jesus Christ—Name. 2. Jesus Christ—Person and offices.
I. Title.
BT590.N2S45 1999
232—dc21   99-27900
                                                               CIP

Edited by Patty Crowley
Interior design by Desktop Miracles

Scripture quotations not otherwise marked are from the HOLY BIBLE, NEW INTERNATIONAL VERSION®. Copyright ©1973, 1978, 1984 by International Bible Society. Used by permission of Zondervan Publishing House. All rights reserved. Other Scriptures are quoted from *The Holy Bible,* Authorized King James Version (KJV), ©1961 by The National Publishing Co.; *The Holy Bible, New King James Version* (NKJV), © 1982 by Thomas Nelson, Inc.; *New American Standard Bible* (NASB), ©1973 by The Lockman Foundation; *New Revised Standard Version Bible* (NRSV), ©1989 by Division of Christian Education of the National Council of the Churches of Christ in the United States of America; and *The Message: The New Testament in Contemporary Language* (*The Message*), ©1994 by Eugene H. Peterson. Italics within Scripture quotations were added by the author for emphasis.

The Semitic Transliterator fonts used to print this work are available from Linguist's Software, Inc., PO Box 580, Edmonds, WA 98020-0580 USA tel (425) 775-1130.

Part of chapter seven has been taken from *My Heart—Christ's Home* by Boyd Munger. =A91986 InterVarsity Christian Fellowship of the USA, revised edition. Used by permission of InterVarsity Press, P.O. Box 1400, Downers Grove, IL 60515.

Chapter two includes a portion of the words to a song by Michael Card: "Immanuel" ©1987 Birdwing Music/Mole End Music. Chapter three includes the words to a song by Michael Card: "The Final Word" ©1987 Birdwing Music/Mole End Music. All Rights Reserved. Used by Permission.

TABLE OF CONTENTS

for Myra

my partner,
my best friend,
my teacher who shows me Jesus

Author's Preface

WHEN I BECAME A CHRISTIAN, I MADE A PUBLIC confession of Jesus that took the following form: "I believe that Jesus Christ is the Son of God." Modeled on Acts 8:37 in the King James Version, this simple statement is an ancient baptismal confession that probably originated in the second or third century.[1]

It has been the work of a lifetime to understand and live that confession. I now make the same confession with deeper insight and conviction than I was able to bring to it as a child of twelve.

Although I could not have articulated it in this way four decades ago, I was using a formula that consisted of a single proper name, Jesus, and two titles, Christ and Son of God. I confessed then and believe still that Jesus is the anointed Redeemer-King promised to the people of Israel through Moses and the prophets and that he is the holy God-man who has provided eternal life to all who will receive it through faith in him.

This book will explore the person and work of Jesus Christ by looking at several—though certainly not all—of the names and titles used of him in Holy Scripture. We will explore the meaning of such titles as High Priest, Messiah, Lord, Lamb of God, and Son of Man.

The goal of this book is to broaden both your awareness of and appreciation for the work of Jesus through a theological exploration of these titles. Each name contributes something unique and useful to a believer's insight into the Son of God. Each also contains a special challenge for understanding our relationship to him. Each constitutes a particular challenge to living out the practical implications of our faith in him.

I hope you enjoy and learn much from the studies ahead. More than that, I hope your life is changed forever by what God reveals to you about Jesus Christ.

"Sir," they said, "we would like to see Jesus."
—*John 12:21*

CHAPTER ONE

JESUS

MATTHEW 1:21

She will give birth to a son, and you are
to give him the name Jesus, because he
will save his people from their sins.

How did you come to have your name? Were you named for a family member? A dear friend of your parents? Some celebrity? If you have children, how did you choose their names?

The choice of a child's name is quite important to most parents. Some names just won't do. Judas Jones, Jezebel Smith, Adolf Hitler Williams—surely nobody in his right mind would attach those names to a child! It would be a cruel and irresponsible thing to do. On the other hand, people have been known to do some pretty weird things in selecting the names of their children.

For example, this short piece in *USA Today*, 8 September 1994, caught my eye when it first appeared and hasn't left my mind since: "George and Tina Rollason say God had nothing to do with the birth of their daughter

1

on July 20, so they gave her a fitting moniker: Atheist Evolution Rollason. The York, Pa., couple say her name is their answer to other parents' use of biblical names. 'There's so many people named Christian, or Christine,' George says. 'This is just one person named Atheist. What the heck's the difference?' The Rollasons have clashed with the school district over angel decorations in the classroom and Bibles in the library."

In some situations, there really is "nothing in a name." But at other times, people like the Rollasons intend a name to be a statement of conviction or perhaps a commitment and pledge about their child's upbringing. In biblical literature, names often have special meaning for someone's spiritual life and destiny. Adam, Abraham, Sarah, Israel— most Bible students know the significance of these God-chosen names to the roles played by the people bearing them.

When the time came for God to put the wheels in motion to bring his grand scheme of redemption to fulfillment, the naming of the child born at Bethlehem was not left for others to decide. The infant born in an animal stall was given a name from on high that would pledge and foreshadow the work he would accomplish.

> This is how the birth of Jesus Christ came about: His mother Mary was pledged to be married to Joseph, but before they came together, she was found to be with child through the Holy Spirit. Because Joseph her husband was a righteous man and did not want to expose her to public disgrace, he had in mind to divorce her quietly.
>
> But after he had considered this, an angel of the Lord appeared to him in a dream and said, "Joseph son of David, do not be afraid to take Mary home as your wife, because what is conceived in her is from the Holy Spirit. She will give birth to a son, and you are to give him the name *Jesus*, because *he will save his people from their sins*." (Matt. 1:18–21)

THE NAME *JESUS*

Jesus is the Greek form of the Old Testament Jewish name *Yeshua*. In English, most of us know the name better in its biblical form as *Joshua*. This Hebrew name was translated into Greek for the Septuagint as *Iēsous*, from which we get our transliteration "Jesus."

Its Commonness

We know the name in the Old Testament principally from Joshua son of Nun, the successor to Moses who led the Israelites into Canaan to possess and occupy it. As Moses was about to end his career, God himself chose his successor: "The LORD said to Moses, 'Now the day of your death is near. Call Joshua and present yourselves at the Tent of Meeting, where I will commission him.' So Moses and Joshua came and presented themselves at the Tent of Meeting" (Deut. 31:14). Upon Moses' death, the people accepted him as their new leader, and his name became established among the great personalities in Israel's history (see Deut. 34:9; Josh. 1:16–18). The name Joshua also appears following the Exile. A high priest named Joshua is the central figure in a dramatic parable of redemption by grace in Zechariah 3:1–9.

Joshua came to be a very popular and common name among Jews of the pre-Christian era. During the period that followed Alexander the Great, the dominance of the Greek language throughout the Mediterranean world caused the name to appear as Jesus. In the writings of Josephus, for example, he names nineteen different men who bore the name Jesus. The name is also found on numerous grave markers and tombs found in and around Jerusalem—sometimes in its Hebrew form *Yeshua* and sometimes in its Greek form *Iēsous*.

In the New Testament literature, the name appears a few times to identify persons other than the Jesus who is central to Christian faith. Although translated as "Joshua" in most English versions, the Greek name of an ancestor of Jesus of Nazareth is, in the original text, *Iēsous* at Luke 3:29. A certain "Jesus, who is called Justus" is associated with Paul in Colossians 4:11. There is even good textual evidence that the full name of the "notorious prisoner" released at the trial of Jesus of Nazareth was Jesus Barabbas (Matt. 27:16–17).[1]

Its Uniqueness

In its older Hebrew form, the name means "Yahweh is salvation" or "Yahweh rescues." It testifies to the power and love of Yahweh. It points all who hear it to look to the Lord for help and redemption. The oldest name known to us that contains the divine name Yahweh, it affirms the uniqueness of Israel's God as the one in whom humankind may safely trust for salvation. It declares that there is no one worthy of comparison to Yahweh. No other name offers what his name promises.

Once a very common name, the name Jesus had become rare as a personal name by the end of the first century. By that time, it had come to be associated with one man to the degree that it was deemed uniquely his. That man, of course, was Jesus of Nazareth, Jesus Christ, or the Lord Jesus. The name came to be held in such deep reverence by Christians that they reserved it for him alone. And unbelievers, whether Jew or Gentile, avoided the name because of its unique association with the one Christians confessed as their Christ and Lord. Following is a discussion on why that happened—and why the name Jesus came to mean something more than its respected etymology and history.

THE NAME AS THEOLOGICAL STATEMENT

When Matthew used the name Jesus while writing of Jesus' birth, he was aware of all the Old Testament background we have just traced. A Jew writing the most Jewish of the four gospels, Matthew knew the significance of names given to important figures in God's sovereign agenda in history. So he certainly did not miss the significance of the angel's words

4

to Joseph, when Mary's husband-to-be was told, "She will give birth to a son, and you are to give him the name Jesus, because he will save his people from their sins" (1:21).

Jesus Saves

What significance would Matthew have seen in the angel's words? What did he mean for his readers to see in them? Most simply stated, the theological significance of Matthew 1:21 is that the angel's words "attribute to Jesus what was formerly reserved for God."[2]

Whereas the name Jesus had till that time meant "Yahweh saves," the birth of the child Jesus would hereafter affirm that "Jesus saves." It was as if the angel had said to Joseph: "Joseph, you have always believed that salvation comes from Yahweh. Certain of your forebears have even testified to that fact by wearing a name that says as much. But in the unique child that Mary will bear, God will be personally present and personally active in saving people. For you and Mary, then, know the heavenly mystery that Jesus is heaven's instrument for salvation to all who will believe in him. God will save all who come to Jesus and receive his favor. This child Jesus will be, in his own person and deeds, the savior to whom others have testified and for whom they have longed!"

Yahweh Come among Us

Jesus is Israel's covenant God, Yahweh, come among us. Jesus is—as we will discuss in the next chapter—*Immanuel*, God with us (see Matt. 1:23). For Christians, the name Jesus does not point to an invisible, enthroned deity who can save—as the name Yahweh did. To the contrary, it names the one in whom God became visible, incarnate, and accessible. It names the one in whom we can be rescued from sin. As Peter would later declare to the Sanhedrin: "Salvation is found in no one else, for there is no other name under heaven given to men by which we must be saved" (Acts 4:12).

This same understanding and affirmation concerning Jesus is found not only in Matthew but in Luke. Without couching the birth narrative in the unfamiliar terms of Hebrew names and their meanings, Luke—a non-Jew writing to non-Jews—relates the announcement of an angel to shepherds in the field this way: "The angel said to them, 'Do not be afraid. I bring you good news of great joy that will be for all the people. Today in the town of David *a Savior has been born to you;* he is Christ the Lord. This will be a sign to you: You will find a baby wrapped in cloths and lying in a manger'" (Luke 2:10–12).

Unlike Islam's claim for Mohammed that he is God's prophet, Christianity makes the claim for Jesus that he is himself God. He is not merely a spokesman *for* God or a prophet telling *about* God. He *is* God! He is God among us. He is God demonstrating his holiness and power in our midst. He is God saving us. So his name is understood as a promise of everything that was fulfilled in his life and ministry and that is even now being preached to the ends of the earth.

A GOSPEL EVENT

Although Jesus made the direct and unambiguous claim to be divine in a number of settings,[3] one of the most intriguing texts on this point is couched in a miracle story in the Gospel of Mark. It is the story of a lame man who was healed dramatically. More important for our purposes, however, it contains a bold claim from Jesus that is either blasphemy or self-disclosure.

Jesus was in Capernaum, and quite a crowd gathered to hear him. The house in which he was teaching a few people quickly became a house that was packed full. And that created a problem for four men who had a friend who was paralyzed. The friends—if not the man himself—had heard of Jesus' miracle-working power and wanted them to meet. Their obvious hope was that the paralyzed man would be made whole.

> Some men came, bringing to him a paralytic, carried by four
> of them. Since they could not get him to Jesus because of the
> crowd, they made an opening in the roof above Jesus and,

after digging through it, lowered the mat the paralyzed man was lying on. When Jesus saw their faith, he said to the paralytic, "Son, your sins are forgiven."

Now some teachers of the law were sitting there, thinking to themselves, "Why does this fellow talk like that? He's blaspheming! Who can forgive sins but God alone?"

Immediately Jesus knew in his spirit that this was what they were thinking in their hearts, and he said to them, "Why are you thinking these things? Which is easier: to say to the paralytic, 'Your sins are forgiven,' or to say, 'Get up, take your mat and walk'? But that you may know that the Son of Man has authority on earth to forgive sins . . . ." He said to the paralytic, "I tell you, get up, take your mat and go home." He got up, took his mat and walked out in full view of them all. This amazed everyone and they praised God, saying, "We have never seen anything like this!" (Mark 2:3–12)

When Jesus and the others in that hot, crowded room witnessed the curiosity of a man being lowered through a hole in the roof,[4] everyone's attention turned toward the paralyzed man. Jesus also saw him, marveled at the faith of those who had gone to such trouble to bring their friend, and said, "Son, your sins are forgiven."

This statement from Jesus has been the source of a great deal of speculation. Some have thought that it shows Jesus attributed all sickness and disability to sin. The larger record of his ministry clearly shows that is not so (see John 9; Luke 13:1–5). Others have speculated that he started as he did in this case because he knew the paralysis of this particular man was due to some sinful behavior. Perhaps, but even that does not necessarily follow.

Jesus always pointed people from their immediate perceived need to their larger need for salvation. Do you remember his conversation with a Samaritan woman at Jacob's well? (John 4). She had come to draw water from the well, and Jesus engaged her in a conversation about "living water" that led to her salvation—and the conversion of many more people from her village. As great as this man's need for bodily healing was, Jesus knew that his—and everyone's—greater need was for spiritual healing. So Jesus' first response to the great faith he had just witnessed was to invite the paralyzed man into the peace of forgiveness.

Before Jesus could go further with the man, his comment about forgiveness stirred many of his hearers to negative thoughts. "Why does this fellow talk like that?" they were saying to themselves. *"Who can forgive sins but God alone?"*

Jesus Claims Deity

Here is a case where Jesus' critics had their premises right but their conclusion wrong. They were absolutely correct in their belief that God alone has the right to forgive sins. They had also heard and understood Jesus to have claimed the right to forgive sins himself when he addressed the paralyzed man. Only one of two conclusions was possible for them to draw: Jesus was either God on earth or guilty of blasphemy. They drew the second conclusion rather than the first.

If Jesus wasn't claiming to be deity here, he could have corrected the "misunderstanding" of his hearers. He could have said, "Oh, please! Don't hear me saying that I have the power to forgive sins personally. I was simply reassuring this poor man that God loves him and wants him to be forgiven." But that isn't what he said! Or he could have said, "Excuse me for leaving the wrong impression, for I certainly don't want to blaspheme. Only God can forgive sins, and I am merely a man among men." But he didn't say that either! He let it stand—as spoken and as understood.

Jesus Claims the Ability to Forgive Sins

What is more, Jesus proceeded to give his bold claim credibility by asking, "Which is easier: to say to the paralytic, 'Your sins are forgiven,' or to say, 'Get up, take your mat and walk'?" In order to understand his question, emphasize the word *say* as you read it. Of course, forgiving sins is a greater, harder, and far costlier thing to God than healing legs. It was going to cost Jesus his life on a Roman cross! But in terms of merely saying those two things in that house on that day, which was easier? As a matter of fact, *saying* "Your sins are forgiven" was easier than "Get up, take your mat and walk" because the latter was testable in a way the former was not. The matter of forgiveness might never get beyond Jesus saying "They are forgiven!" and his critics replying "No they aren't!" And that could have gone on endlessly. If he told a paralyzed man to get up and walk, though, he would be revealed—either as a heaven-verified man in *all* he said (including forgiveness and identity) or as a fraud.

So Jesus turned to the man, told him he was healed, and sent him home. The once-paralyzed man stood up, picked up the mat on which he had been carried, and walked out through the crowd. Jesus wasn't a fraud. He was a healer. He was a truth-teller. He was anything but a blasphemer in saying he could forgive sins. *He was deity among humankind who could save people from their sins!*

Another way of saying all this about him is simply to quote the angel's words to Joseph: "You are to give him the name Jesus, because he will save his people from their sins." Yes, Yahweh saved. And he does so in Jesus. That is why the church in Acts and believers today preach salvation "in the name of Jesus."

The very name of Jesus proclaims his deity. It declares that God loves us—not from a great, safe distance but—up close and personal. It means that we understand much more now about God's nature and saving work. And it means that we can know God.

John Grisham's novel *The Street Lawyer* tells a powerful story. Michael Brock is a young lawyer on the fast track to partnership in an eight-hundred-member firm. But his life gets yanked around by a dramatic hostage event in which he and some of his colleagues are held and threatened by a homeless man. At one point, Brock thinks to himself: "A gun in your face, the clock stops, priorities emerge at once—God, family, friends. Income falls to the bottom. The firm and the career vanish as each awful second ticks by and you realize this could be the last day of your life."[5] Michael Brock abandons his cushy job to be a "street lawyer," an advocate for the homeless.

Like Michael Brock, God left heaven's splendor to become the "Street Savior" of all who will come to him.

We can't climb the stairs that lead to heaven. In spite of the fact that religion has preached self-justification (and self-righteousness!) through law and good works for centuries, the name Jesus reminds us that God came down heaven's stairway and saved us at the end of the street that led from Pilate's judgment hall to Golgotha.

Go to Jesus' cross. Stand with him there. And he will be your defense attorney by whose advocacy—and in whose name—you will be declared righteous.[6]

CHAPTER TWO

IMMANUEL

MATTHEW 1:23

"The virgin will be with child
and will give birth to a son,
and they will call him Immanuel"
—which means, "God with us."

IS THERE SOMEONE YOU MISS TERRIBLY TODAY? A friend who has moved away? A family left behind when you went to college or took a job in a new place? Someone who once had a nurturing, formative role in your life from whom you are now alienated? A person you love who doesn't know it—or worse, who doesn't care? A parent or mate or child who has died? The pain of separation and distance are very real and very terrible.

Is there someone whose pending departure is already causing you sadness? A child who is leaving home for school, military service, or career? A person you once thought you would marry—or whom you *did* marry—who is slipping away, so that you know the relationship isn't going to survive? An important person in your life who is dying?

I don't bring these melancholy thoughts to your mind to make you sad. Please, to the contrary! I am only asking you to realize the impact of separation from someone you love. And the reason I want you to acknowledge the pain of separation is so you can rejoice with me today in the fact that Jesus of Nazareth is Immanuel.

Unfaithful friends abandon you, and the most faithful ones die. Someone who is physically present is sometimes emotionally and spiritually absent. And even those who care and come to you in love are limited in their ability to understand or aid you. Jesus, however, is the believer's forever-present, always-engaged, infinite-in-understanding, limitless-in-power, boundless-in-love, and gracious-to-save God.

No distant, aloof, inaccessible deity is our Jesus! Just listen to these texts from Holy Scripture: "We do not have a high priest who is unable to sympathize with our weaknesses, but we have one who has been tempted in every way, just as we are—yet was without sin. Let us then approach the throne of grace with confidence, so that we may receive mercy and find grace to help us in our time of need" (Heb. 4:15–16). "In him and through faith in him we may approach God with freedom and confidence. I ask you, therefore, not to be discouraged" (Eph. 3:12–13a). "I am convinced that neither death nor life, neither angels nor demons, neither the present nor the future, nor any powers, neither height nor depth, nor anything else in all creation, will be able to separate us from the love of God that is in Christ Jesus our Lord" (Rom. 8:38–39).

But I am getting ahead of myself. For anyone to hear these texts in the fullness of assurance and faith, he or she must know some things about Jesus. So let's go back to the Gospel of Matthew to begin laying a foundation for understanding. My goal in doing so is to make the name Immanuel meaningful enough that you will forever hear it as heaven's assurance that no one who knows and trusts Jesus will ever be left without his presence.

BACKGROUND TO IMMANUEL

In Matthew's account of the birth of Jesus, Mary's pregnancy was explained to a pained and perplexed Joseph as a miracle. Joseph was told that "the child conceived in her is from the Holy Spirit," not some paramour. Mary was indeed still a pure virgin. But she had been selected of God to be the mother of God Incarnate. She would give birth to a son. That holy child was to be given the name "Jesus, because he will save his people from their sins."

At the end of his account of Joseph's dream–vision and before telling of the carpenter's obedience to the angel's instructions, Matthew inserts this explanatory note: "All this took place to fulfill what the Lord had said through the prophet: 'The virgin will be with child and will give birth to a son, and they will call him Immanuel'—which means, 'God with us'" (Matt. 1:22–23).

Isaiah's Use of *Immanuel*

The word Matthew interprets to mean "God with us" appears three times in two Old Testament passages. Both texts are in Isaiah and are set in the context of Yahweh's promised deliverance of the Kingdom of Judah at a time of great national peril. The Northern Kingdom (Israel) was in league with Syria to capture Judah. Judah's king at the time was Ahaz, and he was frightened about his prospects against so formidable a foe. Wicked man that he was, Ahaz knew that he was in no position to claim God's presence and power for deliverance. A word of assurance was nevertheless sent through Isaiah that God would deliver the nation—not for Ahaz's sake but for the sake of the Lord's own faithfulness to his people.

When Isaiah was sent to Ahaz, God offered the king a "sign" that the message was authentic. Ahaz would not even honor the Lord in so desperate a crisis, and so he refused to ask for a sign. Yahweh proceeded to give a sign anyway, for the sake of the nation's reassurance. Thus the famous prophecy: "Then Isaiah said, 'Hear now, you house of David! Is it not enough to try the patience of men? Will you try the patience of my God also? Therefore the Lord himself will give you a sign: The virgin will be with child and will give birth to a son, and will call him Immanuel'" (Isa. 7:13–14).

In the very next chapter, the name Immanuel occurs twice more. Although the Southern Kingdom was to be spared conquest at the hands of the Syria-Israel coalition, it was foretold that Immanuel's land, Judah, would nevertheless one day be conquered by Assyria. Under the image of a flooding Euphrates River, Isaiah warned that Assyria would "sweep on into Judah, swirling over it, passing through it and reaching up to the neck. Its outspread wings will cover the breadth of your land, O Immanuel!" (Isa. 8:8). Then, only two verses later, the name is repeated as an assurance that even so mighty a power as Assyria would not thwart God's sovereign purposes for Judah. So the enemies of Yahweh were told: "Devise your strategy, but it will be thwarted; propose your plan, but it will not stand, for God is with us [Hebrew, *Immanuel*]" (Isa. 8:10).

Matthew Brings Light to Isaiah's Use of *Immanuel*

From this background, Matthew's explanation becomes clear. One writer summarizes it in these words:

> The name of "Immanuel," the son born of the virgin, is to be the watchword for God's people, the word of hope, no matter how desperate conditions become among men. He is the hope because His name means that God is with us. This would indicate that the one born of the virgin is more than man. He is also God. Isaiah 9 would seem to support this, for there the child is called "Mighty God" (Isa. 9:6).
>
> That this interpretation is correct from the Biblical standpoint is made quite clear in the Matthew passage which states that the birth of Jesus by the Virgin Mary fulfills this prophecy from Isaiah (Matt. 1:23). The meaning of Jesus' birth, we are told, is that now God is truly with us in the person of Jesus the Christ.[1]

The very name Immanuel offers a fundamental assurance that believers need in every generation, in every life circumstance. No matter what is happening in this sin-filled world, God is still sovereign and will meet the needs of his people. Regardless of the plans formed against men and women of faith, the one in whom they have placed their faith is a promise-keeper who will never forsake them.

HOW FRIGHTENED PEOPLE BECOME CONFIDENT

If Satan, unfaithful people, or painful life circumstances frighten you, you are not alone. But the God-with-us promise is meant to turn frightened people—as *all* of us are at times—into confident people. People who will not quit. People who will move forward in faith during the darkest times. People who will trust God to see us through hell's plan to destroy us.

Moses' Confidence: "I Will Be with You"

Moses was a man with an erratic past when the Lord confronted him at age eighty and called him to lead the Hebrew people out of their bondage in Egypt. Yahweh spoke to him from a burning bush and told him to go to Pharaoh, demand the freedom of Jacob's descendants, and lead them to a homeland. Right! A murderer who left Egypt four decades ago is going back? A man who had been a privileged prince in the court of Pharaoh but is now only a shepherd of Midian is going to make a political demand of the world's mightiest leader?

Moses asked a perfectly logical question when his commission came: "Who am I, that I should go to Pharaoh and bring the Israelites out of Egypt?" (Exod. 3:11). Here is the answer he received—with special emphasis put on the way that answer begins:

> And God said, "*I will be with you*. And this will be the sign to you that it is I who have sent you: When you have brought the people out of Egypt, you will worship God on this mountain."
>
> Moses said to God, "Suppose I go to the Israelites and say

to them, 'The God of your fathers has sent me to you,' and
they ask me, 'What is his name?' Then what shall I tell them?"
God said to Moses, "I AM WHO I AM. This is what you are to
say to the Israelites: 'I AM has sent me to you.'" (Exod. 3:12–14)

Although this text perplexes many who read it in English, in the
Hebrew language it is really an emphatically beautiful answer to Moses'
question. Four times in rapid succession, forms of the verb "to be" are
used for dramatic effect. "The verbs are first person common *qal*
imperfects of the verb 'to be,' connoting continuing, unfinished
action: 'I am being that I am being,' or 'I am the Is-ing One,' that is, 'the
One Who Always Is.' Not conceptual being, being in the abstract, but
active being, is the intent of this reply. It is a reply that suggests that it is
inappropriate to refer to God as 'was' or as 'will be,' for the reality of this
active existence can be suggested only by the present: 'is' or 'is-ing,'
'Always Is,' or 'Am.'"[2]

What, then, was the answer to Moses' fears? "I will be with you!"
When would God be with him? He already had been! How do you think
he escaped the plan to destroy the male babies of Hebrew mothers? How
do you think he survived when his family hid him along the banks of the
Nile River? Why do you think he was raised in the court of Pharaoh?
How do you think he escaped the police and bounty hunters who tried
to find him after an Egyptian taskmaster was found dead? How do you
think . . . ? Well, you get the point by now.

But when would Yahweh be with Moses in the future? When he stood
in Pharaoh's court? When miracles were needed? When Hebrew children
needed to be spared a death plague? When more than two million Jews
tried to cross natural barriers like rivers? When they needed food and
water? When they grumbled? Yes, yes, *yes!* He would be there in every
one of those circumstances.

And how could Moses believe such a fantastic promise? God revealed
himself by his special covenant name as The Great Always Is, The Great
Is-ing One, The Always Alert and Active One. The promise of this name

and all it implies is the story of the remainder of the Old Testament. God remained present and available to his covenant people. He kept his covenant with them.

Joshua's Confidence: "I Will Be with You"

When Joshua replaced Moses as Israel's national leader, he had his own fears. Would the Lord do through him the same mighty things he had done through Moses? Here is what Yahweh told Joshua when he commissioned him to his work: "No one will be able to stand up against you all the days of your life. *As I was with Moses, so I will be with you; I will never leave you nor forsake you*" (Josh. 1:5). Again, "Have I not commanded you? Be strong and courageous. Do not be terrified; do not be discouraged, for *the* LORD *your God will be with you wherever you go*" (Josh. 1:9).

Our Confidence: God's Presence with Us

The Immanuel concept of God "with" his people was the great mark of distinction for Israel among the many nations of antiquity. Listen, for example, to this conversation between Moses and Yahweh:

> Moses said to the LORD, "You have been telling me, 'Lead these people,' but you have not let me know whom you will send with me. You have said, 'I know you by name and you have found favor with me.' If you are pleased with me, teach me your ways so I may know you and continue to find favor with you. Remember that this nation is your people."
>
> The LORD replied, "My Presence will go with you, and I will give you rest."
>
> Then Moses said to him, "If your Presence does not go with us, do not send us up from here. How will anyone know that you are pleased with me and with your people

unless you go with us? What else will distinguish me and your people from all the other people on the face of the earth?" (Exod. 33:12–16)

What a conversation! God promised Moses that he would go "with" Israel. Moses accepted the promise as Israel's one distinguishing feature among all the nations of the earth. Yahweh would be Israel's Always-Present-Always-Active God!

JESUS WITH US

And so it was natural that the pious Jewish Christian named Matthew would see in the birth, career, and actions of Jesus the full realization of everything that had ever been encapsulated in the name Immanuel.

Making Dreams Come True

The name of the person who wrote the following piece has long since been lost. But it tells the beautiful story of all that would become reality through Immanuel in such wistful, beautiful language. The Jesus who would make all these dreams into realities was the one Matthew saw as "God with us." Indeed, no one else could be such a One.

> That night when in the Judean skies
> The mystic star dispensed its light,
> A blind man moved in his sleep—
> And dreamed that he had sight.

> That night when shepherds heard the song
> Of angelic choiring near,
> A deaf man stirred in slumber's spell—
> And dreamed that he could hear!

That night when in the cattle stall
Slept Child and mother cheek by jowl,
A cripple turned his twisted limbs—
And dreamed that he was whole.

That night when o'er the newborn Babe
The tender Mary rose to lean,
A loathsome leper smiled in sleep—
And dreamed that he was clean.

That night when to the mother's breast
The little King was held secure,
A harlot slept a happy sleep—
And dreamed that she was pure!

That night when in the manger lay
The Sanctified who came to save,
A man moved in the sleep of death—
And dreamed there was no grave.

Matthew's personal experiences of Jesus told him that he was hearing, seeing, and experiencing God in the flesh. And can it be thought insignificant that Matthew's Gospel closes with this distinctive version of the Great Commission: "Go and make disciples of all nations, baptizing them in the name of the Father and of the Son and of the Holy Spirit, and teaching them to obey everything I have commanded you. And surely *I am with you always*, to the very end of the age" (Matt. 28:19–20)?

Through the Holy Spirit

Jesus is the Eternal Immanuel—God with Us—for Christians. Did he appear to leave and return to the Father? Did he seem to finish his work and go into retirement at the Father's right hand? Do you think he is remote and distant to our present situation? Through the indwelling Holy Spirit, Jesus is with his people personally, constantly, and forever (see John 14:16).

What is the Book of Acts but the story of "God with us" in the activity of the church? Some scholars, in fact, suggest calling Acts not The Acts of the Apostles but The Acts of the Holy Spirit. The active Spirit of God turned the community of faith known as the church into the spiritual body of Christ. That church not only experienced the constant presence of Jesus in its own life but had such an impact on the world of the first century that it knew God was still "with us." Today's church must live the same reality in its experience.

GOD CONTINUES TO BE WITH HIS PEOPLE

Jesus Saves

As Immanuel, Jesus is still in the world to save those who come to him. "There is no difference between Jew and Gentile—the same Lord is Lord of all and richly blesses all who call on him, for, 'Everyone who calls on the name of the Lord will be saved'" (Rom. 10:12–13).

One cold day a Christian was walking down the street and noticed that someone had thrown a handful of birdseed on the ground to keep feathered creatures from dying from the wintry blast. Dozens of hungry little sparrows had descended on it for an unexpected feast. As he came closer, the birds became anxious. Another step and they prepared to fly. A step or two more and they all flew away—leaving their banquet table unfinished. The man stopped, looked, and reflected. Why had the sparrows scattered on the wing, when he had no sinister intention toward them? Then it dawned on him: It was not his intention but his person that had scared them. He was so big! The only way he could have walked among those birds without scaring them would have been to become a sparrow himself, fly down among them, and share their existence.

Isn't that the story of the Incarnation? God had spoken and acted on humanity's behalf before. There had never been any intention but love behind his words and deeds. But the thundering, miracle-working prophets had not been able to bring the people back to the Lord. What was left to do? "In the past God spoke to our forefathers through the prophets at many times and in various ways, but in these last days he has spoken to us by his Son, whom he appointed heir of all things, and through whom he made the universe" (Heb. 1:1–2).

Jesus Comforts

God is still at work in Jesus to comfort his people. "Keep your lives free from the love of money and be content with what you have, because God has said, 'Never will I leave you; never will I forsake you'" (Heb. 13:5; see Josh. 1:5).

Michael Card wrote a beautiful song called "Immanuel" that articulates the theme of "God with us." I must have listened to it no less than a hundred times as I wrote this material.

> For all those who live in the shadow of death,
> A glorious light has dawned.
> For all those who stumble in the darkness,
> Behold, your Light has come!
> Immanuel,
> Our God is with us.
> And if God is with us,
> Who could stand against us?
> Our God is with us.
> Immanuel.

Card is a careful student of the Word of God, and many churchgoers could learn more theology listening to his music than by taking notes on their preachers' sermons. He writes, for example, of the fact that Jesus "longs to share in and to be the source of the laughter and the joy we all too rarely know."[3] He speaks of God's presence in his family—even, and especially, in ordinary, "mundane" moments.

> At a totally different time, in the middle of an argument, we've experienced His disturbing presence, which convicted us of failing to be to each other all He would want us to be.
>
> Most incredible, however, are the times we know He is with us in the midst of our daily, routine lives. In the middle of cleaning the house or driving somewhere in the pickup, He stops us both in our tracks and makes His presence known. Often it's in the middle of the most mundane task that He lets us know He is there with us. We realize, then, that there can be no "ordinary" moments for people who live their lives with Jesus.[4]

Jesus Challenges

And Jesus is "God with us" to challenge us to grow in faith, holiness, and service to the Lord. "If you love me, you will obey what I command. And I will ask the Father, and he will give you another Counselor to be with you forever—the Spirit of truth. The world cannot accept him, because it neither sees him nor knows him. But you know him, for he lives with you and will be in you. I will not leave you as orphans; I will come to you" (John 14:15–18).

Archbishop Desmond Tutu won the Nobel Peace Prize in 1984 for his work in helping lead the struggle against apartheid in South Africa. Many of his speeches and writings that tugged on the conscience of the world pressed the "God with us" theme. For example,

> By becoming a real human being through Jesus Christ, God showed that he took the whole of human history and the whole of human life seriously. He demonstrated that he was

the Lord of all life, spiritual and secular, sacred and profane, material and spiritual. . . . 'Our God cares that children starve in resettlement camps, the somewhat respectable name for apartheid's dumping grounds for the pathetic casualties of this vicious and evil system. The God we worship does care that people are condemned to a twilight existence as nonpersons by an arbitrary bureaucratic act of banning them without giving them the opportunity to reply to charges brought against them. I will show this from the Bible. I might add that if God did not care about these and similar matters, I would not worship him, for he would be a totally useless God. Mercifully, he is not such a God.[5]

Yes, mercifully he is *not* such a God. And we know of his compassion for suffering people and of his call for those who are his disciples to address and end suffering in their world where possible in the name of Jesus of Nazareth. "God with us" challenges the best that is within us to do all we can with the worst that confronts us. Otherwise we are unfaithful to the God who has been with, loved, and cared for us in our worst and most hopeless-looking situations.

I once read about a little girl who told her mother, "Mama, I like you better than God."

"Oh, my dear, you mustn't say that," said her startled mother.

"Yes, but really, Mama. I do like you better than God."

Shocked, but perceptive enough to pursue the matter before voicing any more of her concern for such theology, her mother asked gently, "Sweetheart, what makes you say that?"

The child answered simply, "Because I can hug you! And you hug back!"

That little girl put humanity's universal desire to have contact with God in a personal, tangible way into words. A spirit without a body is difficult—if not impossible—for us to imagine. But a real, flesh-and-bones Jesus in the same reality we experience has meaning for us. As Immanuel, Jesus has brought God within hugging distance. And he has hugged us back. He is with us and will be with us forever.

The final benediction of Scripture is this: "The grace of the Lord Jesus be *with* God's people" (Rev. 22:21). The ultimate reality of everlasting life is this: "We will be *with* the Lord forever" (1 Thess. 4:17). Even if there are others you are missing today because of distance, departure, or death, there is one utterly dependable person in whom you can trust. He will never leave you or forsake you. He is Immanuel, God with you always.

CHAPTER THREE

THE WORD

JOHN 1:1

In the beginning was the Word, and the Word
was with God, and the Word was God.

Back in the twenties, an executive of the New York Telephone Company stopped in amazement one night to watch a man wearing a tuxedo climb out of a manhole at the corner of Forty-second Street and Broadway. The well-dressed man turned out to be Baruch Foraker, head of the Bell telephone operation in New York City. Why, on a cold January night, had a Bell executive come out of a Broadway theater and climbed into the manhole in the first place? Was there a major crisis? Had the system broken down?

"I knew there were a couple of my cable splicers working down there," said Foraker. "So I just dropped in on them to have a little chat." It should surprise no one that he became known as the "man of ten thousand friends." Foraker's habit of visiting his employees at their work sites endeared him to them. It was his way of showing them he considered their work important. More than that, it was his way of valuing them as persons.

For anyone who wonders about the Christian view of humankind, here is the answer: God created us in his own image, revealed his will to us across the generations, and finally became one of us.

Yes, God cared enough to *speak* to us. But he cared more than that. He cared enough to back up his words with actions. He loved us enough that—please pardon the play on an expression we use a lot—he put his person where his mouth was. In Jesus, we have not simply more words *from* God or words *about* God; in him, we have God making his word good by his deeds. Jesus, the living Word, is God's fullest, most perfect, and final word on all things related to spiritual life.

BACKGROUND TO THE CONCEPT

Behind our English term *word* lies the Greek word *logos*. It is a theologically rich word that is used in the New Testament because of its background among both Greeks and Jews. Fundamentally, *logos* simply means "word" or "speech." But there is more to it than a simple definition. This word has a history of use as a technical term with philosophic and religious implications that predates Jesus by centuries. It is this background that explains why the Spirit of God led John to use it of Jesus in the prologue to the Fourth Gospel to say that in Jesus "the Word [Greek, *ho logos*] became flesh and made his dwelling among us" (John 1:14).

The Greek Idea

In terms of its Greek background, the Logos motif goes back at least five hundred years before the time of Jesus to Heraclitus of Ephesus. From the 130 fragments of his preserved writings, we know that his chief concern was to understand how order and symmetry could function in the chaos of the world. It seems that his answer was that there is a force of reason, proportion, and ratio that sustains all things. Typical of the Greek philosophers, he understood reality in terms of opposites—health and disease, light and darkness, justice and injustice, good and evil.

For Heraclitus, it was imperative to try to make sense of how these opposite and discordant forces could be maintained with any degree of orderliness. It appears that he took the concepts of speech, ratio, and intelligence that were all contained in the word *logos* and personified them in his use of *Logos* as a technical term. It stood for the orderly function he saw in the universe, an impersonal force "by which all things are steered through all things."[1] Though for him the Logos was imperceptible to the five senses; nevertheless, the intellect could discern it by reflecting on the phenomena experienced through the senses.

Plato, the greatest of all the Greek philosophers, took up the Logos motif a century and a half after Heraclitus and discussed it at some length in a couple of his later dialogues.[2] His view of the world and our knowledge of it was that all things ultimate and real exist in a transcendent, nonphysical realm of "Forms." According to his view, for example, there is a singular and perfect Form that corresponds to everything we experience in the physical, intellectual, and moral world. Thus there is an ideal Form (Greek, *eidē*) for everything from tree to man to lake, from green to wisdom to sharp, and from goodness to truth to kindness. But these perfections are not visible to our physical eyes or discoverable through our senses. We have impressions of them only as they are partially and imperfectly "reflected" in things known to us in this world.

If, as Plato thought, reality exists only in a transcendent world somewhere, how could we possibly attain it? How can we even aspire to it? His answer was that the best tool for pointing us to the Forms is—you guessed it—Logos. The Logos (word, account, description) of such an ideal thing as holiness, beauty, and justice was not identical to its Form, but it was an indispensable means for attaining true and certain knowledge of it. Plato saw his task as a philosopher as prodding men to think deeply about the truly important things through the use of words—principally challenging people to define or describe qualities such as justice or piety—and thereby causing them to rise beyond mere sensory experience toward the real world of Forms.

Aristotle followed Plato's lead and developed his own distinctive way of using the term *logos*. With his interest in rhetoric and logic, it would have been surprising if he had not employed the term extensively. For him, *logos* came to mean a thing's definition, the conclusion to a syllogism, or the total proof of an argument. For Aristotle and the logicians who followed him, it was the bottom line or definitive word on a matter.[3]

In summary, then, the Greek idea about Logos traces back to a time when the term had notions of both a mathematical (ratio, proportion) and a verbal (speech, articulated word) component. The Logos steers the universe and keeps its forces in balance. It points beyond itself to ultimate reality. It gives orderly, true, and articulate accounts of all things important. It urges men to aspire to what is high and holy. Granted, the Logos is not a person in Greek philosophy. It is an impersonal force that pervades all things and gives understanding about their true nature to those who wish to receive it. It is the definition, conclusion, or proof of an argument. The Logos is the "final word" (singular) that summarizes all the other "words" (plural) that have come before it.

The Jewish Perspective

The Jews, on the other hand, were influenced less by philosophers than by prophets. They were immersed in Scripture. Because of the legacy of Alexander the Great, however, the Jews had been forced to learn and use the Greek language from about the fourth century B.C. and later. And this use of Greek as the common tongue for culture, business, and social life in the Mediterranean world soon required the Jews to produce a Greek translation of their Hebrew Bible. Sometime in the third century before Christ, the Septuagint came into being. Probably produced in Alexandria, the intellectual center of the day, it was a translation of the Law, Prophets, and Psalms—the complete canon of Hebrew Scripture—into the Greek language. It was this version of their Bible that was best known by Jews of the first Christian century, particularly by those Jews who lived outside Palestine. It is the Septuagint rather than the Hebrew text of the Old Testament that was used by the apostles and evangelists of the early church and that is quoted most frequently in the New Testament.

From their use of the Septuagint, Jewish people knew the Greek term *logos* in terms of Yahweh's self-revelation. "After this, the *word* of the Lord came to Abram in a vision . . ." (Gen. 15:1). Yet for the God of the Jews to speak was also for him to act, for his word was powerful. "By the *word* of the LORD were the heavens made, their starry host by the breath of his mouth" (Ps. 33:6).

The foundational nature of the word of God to the life of his Covenant People is apparent from the characteristic formula used in the spoken and written messages of the prophets: "Thus says the Lord . . ." or "The word of the Lord came to" such-and-such a spokesman for Yahweh. As the Jewish people looked to their bright prospects for the future in the reign of the Messiah, it could be represented this way: "The law will go out from Zion, the *word* of the LORD from Jerusalem" (Isa. 2:3; see Mic. 4:2).

Furthermore, the Old Testament Targum made "the Word" a familiar designation of God's very person among the Jews. When Hebrew ceased to be the daily spoken language of the Jews following the Babylonian Exile and Hellenistic Era, the sacred biblical texts continued to be read in Hebrew at synagogue services. In order for the people to receive instruction from a text whose language they no longer understood easily, the custom developed of giving a running translation. Such a translation was called a "Targum." At first oral, the various Targums began to be standardized and written down.

Coupled with the fact that Hebrew reverence led the Jews to avoid pronouncing the divine name for fear of breaking the Third Commandment, interpreters providing a Targum would substitute another term to stand in its place. Thus "Blessed One," "Holy One," or even "The Name" might be put in the place of Yahweh's covenant name. One of the terms widely used among the targumists was "the Word." Thus where Exodus 19:17 reports that Moses "led the people out of the camp to meet with God," various Targums known to us read, ". . . to meet the Word of the Lord." As a result, it can be claimed that "wherever people were familiar with the Targum they were familiar with 'the Word' as a designation of the divine."[4]

Philo's Contribution

Against this wider background within Judaism, Philo of Alexandria (circa 20 B.C.–circa A.D. 40) developed a detailed doctrine of the Logos within Jewish thought. Born in Egypt, Philo clearly knew the Greek Septuagint better than the Hebrew (Masoretic) text of the Bible. But he also knew Greek philosophy, particularly Plato. Standing between the Jewish and Greek traditions, he sought to mesh the two. Philo's focal point for the synthesis he attempted is the Logos concept.

Philo used the term *logos* more than thirteen hundred times in his writings that are still available for us.[5] The Logos is the instrument of mediation for a transcendent God who—following the Greek philosophers—was pure spirit being who was unable to have contact with the physical universe he had created.

Furthermore, the Logos is the means by which humankind can approach God. "In his theology the Logos is the manifest and active deity; and in his interpretation of the Scriptures, where God appears to men, converses with them, reveals his will and purpose, it is, according to Philo, of the Logos that all this should be understood."[6]

In Philo's own words, "God's shadow is His Word, which he made use of like an instrument, and so made the world."[7] The Logos/Word is therefore the best hope that humans have for knowing anything about God. By studying his "shadow," we can get a glimpse of his true form or nature. Man is able to free himself from the pull of this world by listening to the Logos, the Word of God. The Word calls us to God.

By now you may be thinking that you've learned more about Heraclitus, Plato, and Philo than you ever cared to know. You may be wondering what relationship there is between tracing out all this Greek and Hebrew information about a single word and its use as a philosophical device. But isn't it apparent why all this is terribly, terribly important?

When John came to write the final of the four Gospels, his intention was to tell the story of Jesus in order to bring men to faith and life in him (John 20:30–31). To whom did he wish to deliver his message? To Jews? To Gentiles? *To both!* Yet there is such a great cultural divide between the two. How could he address both so as to capture their attention and interest? How could he draw in one group of readers without disappointing or alienating the other? The Holy Spirit led him to this solution: *John, open your Gospel by writing about the Logos/Word.*

The single most significant topic for discussion that could serve as common ground for Greeks and Jews to consider the person, work, and claims of Jesus was *the Word*. So John was led by the Spirit to preface his gospel this way: "In the beginning was the Word, and the Word was with God, and the Word was God. He was with God in the beginning. . . . The Word became flesh and made his dwelling among us. We have seen his glory, the glory of the One and Only, who came from the Father, full of grace and truth" (John 1:1–2, 14).

It is no accident that John presents Jesus of Nazareth to his readers by means of a "loaded" term that would catch the attention of any literate person of his time. His or her attention captured, John then proceeds to explain the Christian doctrine of Jesus as the Logos/Word of God. It hardly strains the imagination to think that John had learned the value of such an introduction in his oral presentations of the gospel.

"My Greek friends," John might begin, "perhaps you have heard the philosophers speculate about the Word that steers the universe, makes known the realities that are larger than our mundane existence, puts all of life into balance, or summarizes and completes all the lesser 'words' that have ever been spoken. Would you like to know the Word's identity? My Jewish brothers, what about you? You, too, believe in the power of Yahweh's Word. Philo has told us that the Word reveals God's outline and shadow to us. May I tell you about the Word who has become flesh and who has revealed the fullness of God?" What an attention-grabbing opening!

Modern-Day Concepts

The force of this concept also has a great impact on people of our own time. Words are our means of communication. If there is an idea in your mind that you wish to share with me, how do you go about it? You choose your words carefully. They immediately become the links between your knowledge and my inquiry, your information and my need.

How do people get to know each other well? He calls her on the phone and uses these words: "Uh, this is Bill, and I was hoping you would go to dinner with me tomorrow evening." If Susan accepts, there will be more words during dinner. There will be more phone calls, written notes, and face-to-face conversations. Eventually, there may be the magical, wonderful words passed between them: "I love you." Then there is a marriage ceremony formalized with words. Children are born, named, and taught. Life is shared in all its fullness—with words having started, nurtured, and sustained a relationship that means more than life to them both.

Speak of "words" or "the Word," and we think of the means by which we communicate, get to know each other, and even reveal our deepest secrets to one another. And that is precisely John's point. Wishing to communicate with his human creation, God has done so through Jesus of Nazareth. Learning of Jesus is how we learn of God. The deep things of God that have been secret across the millennia are made known in him. He is no mere shadowy outline of God but the fullness of his grace and truth come in the flesh. In Jesus, the final and complete revelation of God has been personified.

JOHN'S USE: "THE WORD WAS GOD"

John's beautiful Gospel begins with the Logos idea in the forefront. To Greeks, to Jews, to today's readers—Jesus is the Incarnate and Living Word.

The Pre-Flesh Word

First, John writes of Jesus' pre-fleshly existence as the Eternal Word. "In the beginning was the Word, and the Word was with God, and the Word was God. He was with God in the beginning. Through him all things were made; without him nothing was made that has been made. In him was life, and that life was the light of men" (John 1:1–4).

It helps us with the interpretation of John 1:1 to remember that the Greek term *theos* (God/god) is fundamentally a descriptive word rather than a proper name. For the ancient Greeks, this word assigned a thing or person to the highest level of being. Thus, in Christian usage, it can be used to affirm faith in one and only one God (the level of ultimate being) while simultaneously affirming our faith in the distinct personalities of the Trinity—the Father, Son, and Holy Spirit.

To take the word *God* in this opening line of John's Gospel as a personal name for the Father is to create an impossible dilemma. John affirms that Jesus (the Word) was *with* the Father—which is not problematic—and that he *was* the Father—which seems hopelessly problematic. If the word *God* is understood as the family name of deity, however, we may speak of God the Father, God the Son, and God the Holy Spirit without creating utter confusion. Just as there are five persons in my family, there are three persons in the Christian trinity or godhead. So John opens his Gospel with a prologue which affirms: "The Word was *with* the divine family and the Word was *a full-fledged member of* that family."

For Jews and Greeks alike who would read his Gospel, it was obviously important for John to begin with a bold declaration of the deity of Jesus of Nazareth. He affirms here what Jesus will later claim in his own words (see John 10:30–33) and what Christian writers have confessed concerning him from the first century until now (see Phil. 2:6–11). John thus takes up a theme Paul had developed in an epistle written before this Gospel: "God was pleased to have all his fullness dwell in [Jesus]" (Col. 1:19). "In Christ all the fullness of the Deity lives in bodily form" (Col. 2:9).

The police department in Chicago had made very little headway in bringing an end to the violence and gang-related killings in a large inner-city area. Jane Byrne, who was then the city's mayor, had been wrestling with the problem along with her law-enforcement officials. Then she hit upon an astonishing idea. She announced that she and her husband were moving into that very apartment complex. There was widespread support for her idea, and the "experiment" seemed to work. Her identification with that community made a significant difference. Crime was reduced, and new life came back to the community. And that was in spite of the fact that she stayed only briefly in an apartment that was refurbished and under heavy security!

When the Word became flesh in Jesus, it was not the sort of thing that could be dismissed as a publicity stunt to court the voters. It was not a short-duration stay under tight security. It was God living among us for more than thirty-five years, partaking fully of the frailty of our humanity, and being vulnerable to the point of death.

As the personified revelation of God's Word to humanity, Jesus' mission on Earth was to bring "life" to all who are spiritually dead. With John's prologue reminding us of Genesis 1 ("In the beginning . . ."), he pictures the Word's entry into human experience as the breaking of light into darkness. Before physical life could be created in Genesis, light had to be present to sustain it; thus the first thing called into being on the first creative day was light. Similarly, before spiritual life can be created, the light of Jesus' personal holiness, truth, and grace had to penetrate the chaotic darkness of human sin.

The Rejected Word

Second, John calls attention to the startling rejection of the Word by those he came to save.

> The light shines in the darkness, but the darkness has not understood it.
>
> There came a man who was sent from God; his name was John. He came as a witness to testify concerning that light, so that through him all men might believe. He himself was not the light; he came only as a witness to the light. The true light that gives light to every man was coming into the world.
>
> He was in the world, and though the world was made through him, the world did not recognize him. He came to that which was his own, but his own did not receive him. Yet to all who received him, to those who believed in his name, he gave the right to become children of God—children born not of natural descent, nor of human decision or a husband's will, but born of God. (John 1:5–13)

How could this be? Had history not been prepared for the coming of Jesus among men? Had the prophets not foretold the one who would bring all things to their fulfillment? Indeed, had not John the Baptist come as his immediate forerunner? So how could he come into the world and not be received by everyone?

All of us are capable of missing things because of blind spots, preconceptions, and prejudices. And both Greeks and Jews had their preconceived notions of what "greatness" was. When the Word became flesh as a humble man willing to accept the abuses of unbelief, neither Jew nor Greek could acknowledge him!

The Jews, for example, had no concept of a *suffering* servant of Yahweh bringing all things to their fulfillment. They envisioned a king of the glorious order of David—prancing horses, flashing chariots, fleeing Romans. When Jesus came as a carpenter, he did not fit their myopic interpretations of the Old Testament. When Jesus was hung on a Roman cross to die, that was the last straw. The Divine Word dying as a criminal in so horrible a fashion would never do, given their expectation of a triumphant, glorious person who would speak heaven's final word on all things.

The Greeks were less guilty than the Jews of missing Jesus' true identity because of their spiritual blindness. Conditioned as they had been by the great thinkers and writers in their philosophic tradition, they awaited a word from God that would agree with their sound reasoning. Or perhaps that word would come through a great speaker. But it could not come, so they thought, through a Jewish peasant from so unpromising a place as Nazareth in Galilee.

So Jesus was rejected by both! Paul—though he grew up in the Greek city of Tarsus, was born and educated as a Jew. Thus he was an heir to both the Jewish and Greek traditions. Of the rejection of Jesus, he wrote:

> For the message of the cross is foolishness to those who are perishing, but to us who are being saved it is the power of God. For it is written:
>
> > "I will destroy the wisdom of the wise;
> > the intelligence of the intelligent I will frustrate."
>
> Where is the wise man? Where is the scholar? Where is the philosopher of this age? Has not God made foolish the wisdom of the world? For since in the wisdom of God the world through its wisdom did not know him, God was pleased through the foolishness of what was preached to save those who believe. Jews demand miraculous signs and Greeks look for wisdom, but we preach Christ crucified: a stumbling block to Jews and foolishness to Gentiles, but to those whom God has called, both Jews and Greeks, Christ the power of God and the wisdom of God. For the foolishness of God is wiser than

man's wisdom, and the weakness of God is stronger than man's strength. (1 Cor. 1:18–25)

For those persons—whether ancient or modern—who will receive him as the enfleshed Word of God, their blessing is "the right to become children of God." Yet becoming children of God is no matter of human accomplishment but entirely a work of divine grace, for these are "children born not of natural descent, nor of human decision or a husband's will, but born of God." John will fill out this birth theme later in connection with a conversation between Jesus and Nicodemus (see John 3:1-8).

The Redemptive Work of the Fleshly Word

Third, John confesses the Word's redeeming work done while in fleshly form.

> The Word became flesh and made his dwelling among us. We have seen his glory, the glory of the One and Only, who came from the Father, full of grace and truth.
> John testifies concerning him. He cries out, saying, "This was he of whom I said, 'He who comes after me has surpassed me because he was before me.'" From the fullness of his grace we have all received one blessing after another. For the law was given through Moses; grace and truth came through Jesus Christ. No one has ever seen God, but God the One and Only, who is at the Father's side, has made him known. (John 1:14–18)

As surely as John affirmed the full deity of Jesus in the opening verses of his prologue, so here does he affirm with equal boldness his full humanity. God had loved humans enough that he truly "shared in their humanity" (Heb. 2:14). Indeed, anyone who will not confess the genuine humanity of Jesus shares the "spirit of the antichrist" (1 John 4:1–3).

During the time of the Word's experience in flesh, John and other eyewitnesses had seen "his glory, the glory of the One and Only, who came from the Father." Just as Israel's deity once manifested his glorious presence through the tabernacle erected by Moses in the wilderness, he showed his glory even more completely by living briefly in a tabernacle of flesh.

Jesus—the Perfect Revelation of God

As the incarnate and incomparable Word, Jesus was "full of grace and truth." These two qualities are hallmarks of God, and both have been revealed from Eden forward. Prior to Jesus, though, neither—much less *both* simultaneously—had been seen in full measure in a single setting. In Christ, the revelation of God is complete and lacking in nothing.

Jesus has revealed God uniquely, for he alone has full knowledge of the essential divine nature. Theophanies (visible appearances of God to humans) have occurred at various times in history (see Exod. 24:9–10; Deut. 5:24). Thus to say that "no man has ever seen God" is not to say there had been no revelations of deity prior to Jesus but that there had never before been a *completely adequate* revelation before him. So perfect is the revelation of God in Jesus, in fact, that anyone who has seen him has also seen the Father (see John 14:9).

THE MEANING TO US

For people of our time and place in history, knowing Jesus as the Word means at least three things.

Jesus Clarifies the Confusing

First, the vague has become clear and our dreams reality in Jesus. "In the past God spoke to our forefathers through the prophets at many times and in various ways, but in these last days he has spoken to us by his Son, whom he appointed heir of all things, and through whom he made the universe. The Son is the radiance of God's glory and the exact representation of his being, sustaining all things by his powerful word" (Heb. 1:1–3).

Jesus Reveals God

Second, God can be known in personal terms. Michael Card, in his poetic way, says this in his song "The Final Word":

You and me we use so very many clumsy words.
The noise of what we often say is not worth being heard.
When the Father's Wisdom wanted to communicate His love,
He spoke it in one final perfect Word.
He spoke the Incarnation and then so was born the Son.
His final word was Jesus, He needed no other one.
Spoke flesh and blood so He could bleed and make a
    way Divine.
And so was born the baby who would die to make it mine.

And so the Father's fondest thought took on flesh and bone.
He spoke the living luminous Word, at once His will
    was done.
And so the transformation that in man had been unheard
Took place in God the Father as He spoke that final Word.

He spoke the Incarnation and then so was born the Son.
His final word was Jesus, He needed no other one.
Spoke flesh and blood so He could bleed and make a
    way Divine.
And so was born the baby who would die to make it mine.

And so the Light became alive,
And manna became Man.
Eternity stepped into time
So we could understand.

He spoke the Incarnation and then so was born the Son.
His final word was Jesus, He needed no other one.

Spoke flesh and blood so He could bleed and make a
    way Divine.
And so was born the baby who would die to make it mine.

Jesus Validates God's Promises

Third, because of Jesus we know that all God's promises are
dependable. What is your experience of being able to take people at their
word? Has anyone ever failed you? Has anyone ever lied to you? Has anyone ever made a promise in good faith but simply been unable to fulfill
it? Not one of these issues can be a problem with Jesus. He is the final,
guaranteed, and eternally true Word of God. And the salvation and security he has promised you are beyond even Satan's power to overthrow. In
the very person of Jesus, God gave you his Word on it.

A little boy named Timothy wanted to give his grandmother a special
gift one Christmas. Because her Bible was so worn that loose pages
occasionally fell out, he decided to save his money to buy her a new
one. So he saved as much as he could, and his parents finished out the
amount he would need to buy her a beautiful new Bible.

Timothy wanted to write something special to his beloved grandmother on the flyleaf of the Bible, but he was not certain what to say. So
he decided to copy what he had seen in a book his father had received
from a friend and author earlier that year.

His grandmother was thrilled to receive the new Bible but was amused
by this inscription from her grandson: "To Grandma, compliments of
the author."

In Jesus, we have received the words, love, and life of God—
compliments of the Author!

CHAPTER FOUR

LAMB OF GOD

JOHN 1:29

*The next day John saw Jesus coming toward him
and said, "Look, the Lamb of God,
who takes away the sin of the world!"*

T HE LATE NORMAN VINCENT PEALE ONCE SAID this about humility: "Humble people don't think less of themselves; they just think about themselves less." If you ever should be in search of a biblical model of humility, let me suggest that you study that noble virtue in John the Baptist.

John's ministry had been predicted by the last of the writing prophets, Malachi. Thus like going to a good movie and being drawn to its sequel by a few clips from it shown as a coming attraction, the Old Testament closes with a preview of the Messiah's forerunner: "'See, I will send my messenger, who will prepare the way before me. Then suddenly the Lord you are seeking will come to his temple; the messenger of the covenant, whom you desire, will come,' says the LORD Almighty" (Mal. 3:1; see 4:5–6).

Not one of the four Gospel writers discussed the work of Jesus without paying some notice to the career of John. Surely they were influenced to their high estimation of him by Jesus' emphatic statement: "I tell you the truth: Among those born of women there has not risen anyone greater than John the Baptist" (Matt. 11:11).

Did John believe himself to be a prophet from God? Did he know the Old Testament spoke of him? Did he know he had the critical task of preparing people for the arrival of Christ? Indeed, he knew all these things. But here was his estimate of himself and his importance: "After me will come one more powerful than I, the thongs of whose sandals I am not worthy to stoop down and untie. I baptize you with water, but he will baptize you with the Holy Spirit" (Mark 1:7–8). When John's disciples eventually became distraught that Jesus was drawing larger crowds than their master, here was his response: "He must become greater; I must become less" (John 3:30).

Does that sound like someone with a poor, unhealthy self-image? To the contrary. It is the humble response of a man incredibly secure in his perception of himself and his role in the divine plan. It was never the case that he thought less of himself; it was simply that he thought less about himself than Jesus. What a marvelous example of humility in a servant of God.

It is from the lips of John the Baptist that we hear another of the names given to Jesus in Scripture: Lamb of God.

TWO BIBLICAL THEMES

One of the most dramatic stories in the Bible has one of its characters asking for a lamb. Many ceremonies of the Jewish religion centered on the offering of a lamb in sacrifice. Both these facts are important as background to the title "Lamb of God" that John assigned to Jesus of Nazareth. The New Testament presents Jesus as the ultimate provision of a sacrificial lamb.

Substitution

The story that has someone asking for a lamb is the touching father-son episode involving Abraham and Isaac.

Some time later God tested Abraham. He said to him, "Abraham!"

"Here I am," he replied.

Then God said, "Take your son, your only son, Isaac, whom you love, and go to the region of Moriah. Sacrifice him there as a burnt offering on one of the mountains I will tell you about."

Early the next morning Abraham got up and saddled his donkey. He took with him two of his servants and his son Isaac. When he had cut enough wood for the burnt offering, he set out for the place God had told him about. On the third day Abraham looked up and saw the place in the distance. He said to his servants, "Stay here with the donkey while I and the boy go over there. We will worship and then we will come back to you."

Abraham took the wood for the burnt offering and placed it on his son Isaac, and he himself carried the fire and the knife. As the two of them went on together, Isaac spoke up and said to his father Abraham, "Father?"

"Yes, my son?" Abraham replied.

"The fire and wood are here," Isaac said, "but where is the lamb for the burnt offering?"

Abraham answered, "God himself will provide the lamb for the burnt offering, my son." And the two of them went on together.

When they reached the place God had told him about, Abraham built an altar there and arranged the wood on it. He bound his son Isaac and laid him on the altar, on top of the wood. Then he reached out his hand and took the knife to slay his son. But the angel of the LORD called out to him from heaven, "Abraham! Abraham!"

"Here I am," he replied.

"Do not lay a hand on the boy," he said. "Do not do

anything to him. Now I know that you fear God, because you have not withheld from me your son, your only son."

Abraham looked up and there in a thicket he saw a ram caught by its horns. He went over and took the ram and sacrificed it as a burnt offering instead of his son. So Abraham called that place The LORD Will Provide. And to this day it is said, "On the mountain of the LORD it will be provided." (Gen. 22:1–14)

The only person happier than Isaac to see a sheep caught by its horns in a thicket that day was Abraham. He had fathered Isaac in his old age, had doted on the boy, and believed that all Yahweh's promises to him— about descendants, a nation, and a homeland—centered on him. He must have been in anguish of spirit over everything going on in this episode. To his eternal credit, however, he got up early on the appointed day, set off for Mount Moriah, and had no idea of being anything other than obedient to God's command.

From the perspective of the New Testament, we are told this about Abraham's faith in this story: "By faith Abraham, when God tested him, offered Isaac as a sacrifice. He who had received the promises was about to sacrifice his one and only son, even though God had said to him, 'It is through Isaac that your offspring will be reckoned.' Abraham reasoned that God could raise the dead, and figuratively speaking, he did receive Isaac back from death" (Heb. 11:17–19).

Where did that ram come from? Did a sheep just happen to get caught in that thicket on that mountain on that day? Or did the Lord graciously provide it to replace Isaac on the altar? Abraham named the mountain on which he had built an altar for Isaac and where he wound up offering a lamb as a substitute for him "Jehovah-jireh" (KJV) or "The LORD Will Provide." That means he didn't regard the ram in the thicket as a lucky coincidence. In the name he gave that site, he affirmed his faith in the grace of God that spared his Son of Promise and provided a sacrificial lamb in his place.

Indeed, God had never intended to take Isaac's life that day. The whole affair had been a test of Abraham's depth of trust in Yahweh. In other settings and on other days, Abraham had been weak or outright faithless. On this day, however, he was faithful to the ultimate degree. It is from this episode above all others that he received the name Father of the Faithful. When he was tested on Mount Moriah, he passed with flying colors.

Propitiation

Countless Old Testament rituals and offerings involved the slaughter of a lamb on an altar dedicated to Yahweh. These sacrifices had to do with atonement rituals.

The word *atonement* is one of a very few theological terms that can be explained in a helpful way through its English form. It signifies reconciliation and puts people at one (or, at-one-ment). The Hebrew and Greek words beneath this term in our English Bibles combine to point to the purging of defilement and the restoration of peace between humankind and deity.

Yet the word *propitiation* (KJV, NASB, or "atoning sacrifice," NIV) is neither used quite so often nor understood quite as well. Tied closely to the issue of atonement, it denotes turning away wrath by the offering of a gift. It points to something that makes a person inclined to treat you gently and graciously when you have acted in a way that deserves punishment. Some modern students of the Bible don't like the term *propitiation* because they say it implies pagan notions about fickle gods who need humoring and prefer instead the term *expiation* (NRSV). The difference in these two words may be stated concisely by saying that an offended or angry person may be propitiated (appeased), whereas a sin or crime is expiated (removed). Of course, it is easy to see that they do not cancel out one another.

In light of everything the Bible teaches about sin, however, it seems best to retain the notion of propitiation as primary. Because God is holy, he is unalterably opposed to sin. "God is a righteous judge, a God who expresses his wrath every day" (Ps. 7:11). While he may be "slow to anger," he is nevertheless capable of intense anger against evil and its perpetrators. Thus David wrote this: "You have rejected us, O God, and burst forth upon us;

you have been angry—now restore us!" (Ps. 60:1). And Paul wrote of the "wrath of God" that is both revealed in the form of certain consequences people suffer in this life for their sinfulness and is being stored up against the impenitent for the day of final Judgment (Rom. 1:18, 24, 26, 28; 2:5). The truth of the matter is that God's anger at sin is as justified as his joy over the initial creation; his wrath is as holy as his love.

The Old Testament sacrificial system taught the means by which a sinful man or woman could approach a holy God. Since God's anger had been aroused and his wrath made just by sinful deeds, he or she was justified in being afraid to approach the Lord. Because Yahweh had revealed himself as compassion and kindness, however, that same frightened worshiper was invited to come before the Lord with a sacrifice God himself had provided. "The life of a creature is in the blood, and I have given it to you to make atonement for yourselves on the altar; it is the blood that makes atonement for one's life" (Lev. 17:11).

When the individual Israelite approached Yahweh, he brought a sacrifice of atonement and propitiation. When an Israelite family prepared to observe the annual Passover Feast, a sacrifice was killed, eaten together as a family, and its blood sprinkled on the entrance to their house. When the whole nation observed its annual Day of Atonement, still another animal was killed and its blood sprinkled on the mercy seat of the Ark of the Covenant within the temple's Holy of Holies.

In Jesus Christ, the terms *substitution* and *propitiation* come to their climax and fulfillment. In Jesus Christ, the progression reaches its end. "The progression is this: one sacrifice for one individual, one sacrifice for one family, one sacrifice for one nation, one sacrifice for the world. The way to God's presence is now open to anyone who will come, a fact symbolized by the rending of the veil of the temple (which separated the Holy of Holies from the rest of the temple) at Christ's death."[1]

THE BAPTIZER'S ANNOUNCEMENT ABOUT JESUS

John the Baptizer came on the scene when messianic hope was at a fever pitch among the oppressed Jews of Roman-occupied Palestine. He appeared, drew huge crowds, and naturally attracted the notice of the religious establishment. He called everyone who heard him to repentance in view of the Messiah's nearness. In connection with that call, however, was hope. The Messiah would soon appear!

When the priests sent messengers to inquire about his identity (and intentions), he flatly said he was not the Messiah and had no personal illusions of grandeur. The humble man who knew his place in relation to the Christ wanted no one to confuse him with the One whose way he had come to prepare (John 1:19–20). Pressed to identify himself, John quoted Isaiah 40 about the forerunner of Israel's Messiah (John 1:23).

John had baptized Jesus in the Jordan River several weeks earlier, so he knew his true identity (Matt. 3:13–17; see John 1:32-34). Waiting for the right moment to reveal Jesus to others as the long-awaited Redeemer of Israel, John saw him on a certain day and sensed that the time for secrecy had passed. The Passover Festival was close (see John 2:13), so his method of referring to Jesus was natural. Although he was a prophet and not a priest, John knew the importance of sacrifice in the divine scheme. "The next day John saw Jesus coming toward him and said, 'Look, the Lamb of God, who takes away the sin of the world! This is the one I meant when I said, "A man who comes after me has surpassed me because he was before me"'" (John 1:29–30).

"Look, the Lamb of God, who takes away the sin of the world!" What the blood of millions of animals had anticipated, the blood of Jesus secures. In place of the types and shadows of the old covenant, believers in Christ "have been made holy through the sacrifice of the body of Jesus Christ once for all" (Heb. 10:10). In his Gospel,[2] first epistle,[3] and revelation,[4] the apostle John affirms Jesus to be the voluntary, substitutionary, and propitiatory Lamb of God.

Going back to the story of Abraham and Isaac, do you remember where the altar was built and the animal slain? Mount Moriah is mentioned only one other time in the Bible. Unless there were two places with the same name, the place of Abraham's altar was the same one where Israel's temple later stood. "Then Solomon began to build the temple of the LORD in Jerusalem on Mount Moriah" (2 Chron. 3:1). That means, of course, that Isaac was prepared for death and then substituted for by a lamb near the very place where Jesus would be raised on a Roman cross! The substitution provided for Isaac foreshadowed the substitution of Jesus as the Lamb of God for all!

If you can bear to do so, go with me to Jonesboro, Arkansas, on March 24, 1998. Go to Westside Middle School. Let your mind be there in the early morning. Children are laughing, making excuses about homework, and exchanging gossip. But you are there before the fire alarm is pulled and children walk outside into a hail of bullets.

A thirty-two-year-old English teacher is doing the one job that above all others she has aspired to in life. Shannon Wright attended Westside, earned a college degree, and dreamed of teaching in the school she once attended. And here she is Tuesday morning with her students. Explaining nouns and verbs. Correcting grammar. Trying to teach eleven-, twelve-, and thirteen-year-old students to use language correctly.

After a full morning, she enjoys her lunch break. It is a time to be still, to relax, to refocus for her afternoon classes. Just as she finishes lunch and moves her students back to the classroom, the fire alarm sounds. She knows what to do. The school periodically rehearses. In fact, she's probably telling herself there is nothing to worry about. *It's just another of those required drills. They get us ready—just in case there should ever be a real emergency at Westside Middle.*

But that Tuesday turned out to be that dreaded real emergency. No sooner had Mrs. Wright gotten outside than the pop-pop-popping sounds started. Firecrackers? No, bullets! And to her horror she saw children being hit. They were screaming, falling to the ground, bleeding! Then she saw a thirteen-year-old girl directly in the line of fire. So she did what her relatives and coworkers said they would have expected of her. She selflessly put her own body between the little girl and the deadly missiles. Two bullets struck, killing her.

"She loved kids," said her husband, Mitchell. "I'm sure that if she thought someone was trying to hurt one of her kids, she would try to protect them."

God, knowing that someone was trying to hurt—no, *destroy eternally*—the creatures he had made in his own likeness, threw himself in harm's way for their sake. He took the deadly blow that was headed for your soul so you could be spared. I will never understand how two children could kill four of their classmates and one of their teachers in Jonesboro that day. But I hope never to forget the glimpse that Shannon Wright's death has given us of what Jesus did at Calvary. Just as she put her body in the line of fire and saved a child from death, so Jesus went to the cross to save me from the just fate I deserved.

The High Price of Propitiation

As to the propitiation theme, Jesus' death as the Lamb of God was a propitiatory death that satisfied the demand of holiness in relation to sin. His death not only expiated (removed) sin but also propitiated (appeased) a grieved deity in order to make possible the restoration of fellowship between God and man. "He is the atoning sacrifice (propitiation, NASB) for our sins, and not only for ours but also for the sins of the whole world" (1 John 2:2). One of the most familiar messianic texts of the Old Testament points to this aspect of the saving work of Jesus: "He was pierced for our transgressions, he was crushed for our iniquities; the punishment that brought us peace was upon him, and by his wounds we are healed" (Isa. 53:5; see 1 Pet. 2:24). God's wrath has been turned away from those who are in Christ. Although we have done things that merit punishment, Jesus' death has permitted God to treat us with mercy and gentleness.

My friend Phillip Morrison tells about a decision his grandchildren made to learn about nature and country life through the 4-H Club. With their parents' permission, they set up a project with two lambs—Molly and Sarah. They were so tiny when they got them that they had to feed them milk from bottles. They picked them up, held them, stroked them. They bathed them and combed their wool. When they were a little larger, Emily and Joe fed them sweet clover from their hands. It was a wonderful experience for them.

As sheep will do, though, Molly and Sarah got bigger—too big to pick up, too big to have in the house, too big to keep as pets. So the animals were sold. With good experiences behind them and having learned some important lessons, two teenagers moved on to their next adventures.

One evening at the dinner table, Joe was shoveling down one of the best meals he had ever eaten. "This is really good!" he offered his mom. "What's this meat?"

"Leg of lamb," she replied—and a hush fell over the room. Everyone stopped eating. Bites already in progress seemed to hang in everyone's throat.

"Molly! Sarah!" someone finally said. No, they weren't eating their pets. But the thought struck them that somebody somewhere was—or soon would be. When Phillip was told that family story, he says it dawned on him that the lambs carried to the altar at Israel's temple were surely someone's "pets" on at least some occasions. Some worshipers could afford to buy a sacrificial animal from temple salesmen, but many had to bring a lamb from their own little flocks. For the poor, there may have been only one or two or three animals in their "flock." So offering that animal on an altar would not have been a business transaction or ritual. It would have been parting with something dear and precious—an animal you had fed, bathed, and carried in your very own arms. Seeing it offered for your atonement would have made you understand how terrible sin is and would have driven home to you the high price of a propitiation.

The blood of an animal could not really satisfy the demand of justice, however, for it was not an *equivalent* life to the one for which atonement was being made. At best, it was a shadow of how sin would eventually be forgiven (see Heb. 10:1–4). Humans are in the image of God, but animals do not bear that distinguishing feature. Thus someone had to be found who—like the sacrificial lambs under the Law of Moses—was utterly free of blemishes and defects. Jesus and Jesus alone could fill that role.

What a high price for heaven to pay for our transgressions and iniquities! In the person of Jesus of Nazareth, God himself had to be offered on the altar for us! The Prince of Glory had to lay aside his privilege, experience the frailties of humanity and the ravages of sin, and die a propitiatory death. Otherwise the wrath of God would have been executed against us. Now that wrath has been turned away, for Christ has been sacrificed as our propitiation. "It was not with perishable things such as silver or gold that you were redeemed from the empty way of life handed down to you from your forefathers," Peter wrote, "but with the precious blood of Christ, a lamb without blemish or defect. He was chosen before the creation of the world, but was revealed in these last times for your sake" (1 Pet. 1:18–20).

LOOK, THE LAMB OF GOD!

See Jesus now as *your* substitute. Our great provider-God (Jehovah-jireh) has provided what was needed for your sake. You were in the way of a coming deathblow—the knife blade was already raised above your head! But the blow headed for you was absorbed by another! "God made him who had no sin to be sin for us, so that in him we might become the righteousness of God" (2 Cor. 5:21).

See Jesus turning away God's wrath from *you*. Yes, a holy God is justly angry at sin and those who perpetrate its evil deeds and consequences. "In the pagan perspective, human beings try to placate their bad-tempered deities with their own paltry offerings. According to the Christian revelation, God's own great love propitiated his own holy wrath through the gift of his own dear Son, who took our place, bore our sin and died our death. Thus God himself gave himself to save us from himself."[5]

Never blush to confess your faith in the sufficiency of Jesus, the one who bears the name Lamb of God for our sakes. The humble John disclaimed the honor some were ready to assign him and pointed instead to Jesus as the Worthy One. At the same time, he named the terrible role Jesus would have to assume to save us. He would have to become a lamb, a sacrificial lamb, the Lamb of God to take away the sin of the world.

A religious service was being held at the Golden Gate Exposition in San Francisco. Several people in the audience became aware that the man

51

delivering the primary address was not preaching an orthodox gospel. Although a gifted speaker, he derided the idea of something so ghastly as a bloody corpse being required by the God of the Bible for our salvation.

Ruth Marsden relates how, when his speech was ended, a timid, elderly lady stood up in the midst of the crowd and softly began singing the great old hymn *There Is a Fountain* by William Cowper as a heartfelt rebuke to the modernist clergyman's remarks. Silence fell over the crowd as they heard the faint-but-familiar words:

> There is a fountain filled with blood,
> Drawn from Immanuel's veins;
> And sinners plunged beneath that flood,
> Lose all their guilty stains.

Before she could begin the second stanza, around a hundred people rose to join her to sing:

> Dear dying Lamb, Thy precious blood
> Shall never lose its power,
> Till all the ransomed church of God
> Be saved to sin no more.

By the time she reached the third verse, nearly a thousand Christians were on their feet all over the audience and singing that wonderful song of faith. The triumphant, thrilling strains rang out loud and clear:

> E'er since by faith I saw the stream
> Thy flowing wounds supply,
> Redeeming love has been my theme,
> And shall be till I die.

Many, many people were deeply moved that day as a humble believer stood up for her Lord. As related by some of them, the very light of heaven seemed to fall on her face as she gave her testimony to the Lamb of God by whose blood she had found peace.

In Jesus Christ, you can have the same gift.

TRIUMPHAL PASSOVER LAMB

R E V E L A T I O N   5 : 1 2

Worthy is the Lamb,
who was slain, to receive power
and wealth and wisdom and strength
and honor and glory and praise!

JOHN THE BAPTIST IDENTIFIED JESUS AS "the Lamb of God, who takes away the sin of the world" (John 1:29). With the time for the annual Jewish Passover drawing near (see John 2:13), it was significant both to John and to his hearers that Jesus should be identified that way.

Exodus 12 gives the historical setting for Passover. The Israelites were in cruel bondage to the Egyptians, but God had begun acting on their behalf through Moses. The man who would later receive the Ten Commandments on Mount Sinai was told to challenge the powerful Pharaoh in Yahweh's name. "Let my people go!" was the Lord's word to Egypt's leader. As an earthly ruler continued to harden his heart against the cosmic ruler, contests of power between the false gods of Egypt and the living God of the Jews moved toward one final plague against the land.

These were Moses' words to Pharaoh: "This is what the LORD says: 'About midnight I will go throughout Egypt. Every firstborn son in Egypt will die, from the firstborn son of Pharaoh, who sits on the throne, to the firstborn son of the slave girl, who is at her hand mill, and all the firstborn of the cattle as well. There will be loud wailing throughout Egypt—worse than there has ever been or ever will be again. But among the Israelites not a dog will bark at any man or animal.' Then you will know that the LORD makes a distinction between Egypt and Israel" (Exod. 11:4–7).

The way Yahweh showed the "distinction" he made between Egypt and Israel—rebellious oppressors and the Chosen People—was clear on that fateful night. He had instructed Moses to have the head of every household take an unblemished lamb, kill and eat it, and put its blood on the top and sides of the door. The salvation promise was put in these words: "The blood will be a sign for you on the houses where you are; and when I see the blood, I will pass over you. No destructive plague will touch you when I strike Egypt" (Exod. 12:13).

It is from that event of God's "passing over" the houses marked with blood that the Feast of Passover is named. The issue that night was not the size or style of the house; the issue was *blood*. The issue that night was not male or female, young or old; the issue was *blood*. The issue that night was not even good or bad, pious or wicked; the issue that night was *the blood of a lamb* strategically placed around the door of the house. All who were on the inside were saved. All on the outside were under judgment.

STANDING UNDER THE BLOOD

Jesus is our Passover Lamb. Paul wrote, "For Christ, our Passover lamb, has been sacrificed" (1 Cor. 5:7). For the sake of his blood, God "passes over" the sin of believers and spares just judgment against them. When the Holy God of heaven looks down on us Earthlings—rich and poor, males and females, Asians and Westerners, mature and naive, good and bad—who have consented to stand under the blood of Christ, he is reminded of the cross. Because Jesus was offered on that cross as the

Lamb of God to take away the sin of the world, those who stand in that blood-protected place are exempted from judgment. We go free when we deserve to be nothing better than slaves! We live when we should die!

What a price Jesus paid as the *sacrificial* lamb for my sake. I will never be able to take it in. I shall never be able to say enough in his praise. I don't have the ability to give him the service he deserves. It is of grace— totally of grace that he saves. But there is more to the story.

THE TRIUMPHAL LAMB

Jesus is the lamb taken to the slaughter without protest or resistance. He is the compliant, submissive Savior. But he is also the *Triumphal* Lamb who stands now in glory to receive our praise and adoration. He is no longer nailed to a tree. What did the angel tell the women at the tomb on that first Easter morning? "He has risen!" (Mark 16:6). He is alive! He reigns forevermore!

When John was on the prison island Patmos near the end of the first century, the Lord Jesus—both for John's own sake and for the sake of those discouraged saints back on the mainland of Asia Minor—gave him a series of apocalyptic visions. Those visions took John from the mundane to the glorious, from dismay to ecstasy. He was allowed to see beyond the moment into the future.

Surely you've been in situations where you wished you could see the outcome of some crisis. If you believe things will turn out all right, you can endure anything in the meanwhile. If you give way to despair, there is no point in hanging on any longer. Give in, give over, give up! Accept a cruel fate and die!

A little over a month before he died, the Existentialist writer Jean-Paul Sartre looked into the abyss of his uncertain future. Fighting against the despair so evident in his novels, he said he strongly resisted such negative feelings for himself. He would say to himself, "I know I shall die in hope." Then, in profound sadness, the atheist lamented, "But hope needs a foundation."

Hope for the Suffering

Job had suffered terrible losses. He was suffering terribly and was expecting to die soon. He was experiencing such a range of feelings—confusion, dread, anger, and despair. But above all these was hope. He kept believing that God loved his children. He kept affirming that God does what is right.

He expressed this groping-for-understanding faith: "I know that my Redeemer lives, and that in the end he will stand upon the earth. And after my skin has been destroyed, yet in my flesh I will see God; I myself will see him with my own eyes—I, and not another. How my heart yearns within me!" (Job 19:25–27).

In John's day, it was not simply one man who was suffering but an entire generation of the church that was under siege. The Roman Empire had made Christians into nonpersons. It was hounding, arresting, and persecuting people for the "crime" of faith in Jesus of Nazareth. The last living apostle had been taken into custody and isolated from the frightened Christians who were looking to him for instruction and encouragement. Would the infant church be able to survive this ordeal?

Answers for an Anxious Church

In the apocalyptic visions given to John, he saw a scroll in the hand of God the Father. That book contained the answers to a frightened church's anxious questions. Written front and back on the scroll were the secrets to the future. Sealed with seven seals, God himself knew its contents. When John first saw the book and discerned its contents, he was excited about getting answers about the future. Then, as an angel asked this question, John's excitement turned into gloom: "Who is worthy to break the seals and open the scroll?" (Rev. 5:2). When no one could be found worthy to go to the throne and receive the scroll from God, John began to weep. There was no human agent worthy to receive and reveal the mind of God.

At that point in the narrative, one of the twenty-four elders around the throne of God said, "Do not weep! See, the Lion of the tribe of Judah, the Root of David, has triumphed. He is able to open the scroll and its seven seals" (Rev. 5:5). That is messianic imagery from the Old Testament (see Gen. 49:9–10). So John looks, expecting to see the powerful ruler who would come in power and might to scatter the enemies of the people of God and establish righteousness on Earth. But the imagery is changed in a surprising fashion to reveal the one who is worthy above all others.

Then I saw a Lamb, looking as if it had been slain, standing in the center of the throne, encircled by the four living creatures and the elders. He had seven horns and seven eyes, which are the seven spirits of God sent out into all the earth. He came and took the scroll from the right hand of him who sat on the throne. And when he had taken it, the four living creatures and the twenty-four elders fell down before the Lamb. Each one had a harp and they were holding golden bowls full of incense, which are the prayers of the saints. And they sang a new song:

> "You are worthy to take the scroll
>   and to open its seals,
> because you were slain,
>   and with your blood you purchased men for God
>   from every tribe and language and people and nation.
> You have made them to be a kingdom and priests to
>   serve our God,
>   and they will reign on the earth."

Then I looked and heard the voice of many angels, numbering thousands upon thousands, and ten thousand times ten thousand. They encircled the throne and the living creatures and the elders. In a loud voice they sang:

"Worthy is the Lamb, who was slain,
to receive power and wealth and wisdom and strength
and honor and glory and praise!" (Rev. 5:6–12)

God's Purposes Fulfilled by His Blood

God's purposes from eternity past have come to their fulfillment in Jesus Christ. The shadowy anticipations and types of the Old Testament have become reality in him. The Lamb of God who takes away the sin of the world for John the Baptist is the Lamb of God who has triumphed over death for John on Patmos. Prepare-the-way John announces Jesus as the one who is coming for the sake of being laid on the altar of the cross. Hold-the-faith John is permitted to see him as the one who has conquered death and who holds out the hope of victory over that enemy to all who follow him.

John, describe the lamb you see! Why, he has death marks across his throat—but he is standing. He is alive! He has triumphed over death! In this Worthy and Triumphant Lamb, we see the fullness of God's purposes realized for humankind!

> By this one stroke of brilliant artistry John has given us the key to all his use of the Old Testament. . . . Throughout the welter of Old Testament images in the chapters that follow, almost without exception the only title for Christ is the Lamb, and this title is meant to control and interpret all the rest of the symbolism. It is almost as if John were saying to us at one point after another, "Wherever the Old Testament says 'Lion,' read 'Lamb.'" Wherever the Old Testament speaks of the victory of the Messiah or the overthrow of the enemies of God, we are to remember that the gospel recognizes no other way of achieving these ends than the way of the Cross.[1]

The Lion-Lamb Jesus was worshiped with this song: "You are worthy to take the scroll and to open its seals." Please notice that it begins with the same words as those offered to God the Father one chapter earlier: "You are worthy" (Rev. 4:11). If the Creator-God and the Lion-Lamb are worshiped by the same "living creatures" (four creatures representing all of creation) and the twenty-four elders (representing the total covenant community), what are we to conclude? Both share the status of deity, and both are worthy of homage and adoration.

By virtue of Jesus' death, his blood has purchased men for God (see 1 Pet. 1:18–19). By virtue of his status as deity, those belonging to him constitute a "kingdom and priests to serve our God, and they will reign on the earth."

RESURRECTION WORTHINESS OF JESUS

The Son of God

Because of Jesus' resurrection from the dead, we know he is who he claimed to be. He is the unique and incomparable Son of God. Through the prophets, God promised a number of things "regarding his Son, who as to his human nature was a descendant of David, and who through the Spirit of holiness was declared with power to be the Son of God by his resurrection from the dead: Jesus Christ our Lord" (Rom. 1:3–4).

His Atoning Blood

Because of Jesus' bodily resurrection, we know that those who are under his blood are saved. Slain as our Passover, he has been raised as proof that his sacrificial death was accepted as a full atonement. "He was delivered over to death for our sins and was raised to life for our justification" (Rom. 4:25).

A Message for the World

Because of the resurrection of Christ, there is gospel for us to share with the world today. The Easter faith is bogus without the Easter event. Only because he has been raised to life never to die again does the persecuted church of the first century or today's church have a message for the world.

> For what I received I passed on to you as of first importance: that Christ died for our sins according to the Scriptures, that he was buried, that he was raised on the third day according to the Scriptures, and that he appeared to Peter, and then to the Twelve. After that, he appeared to more than five hundred of the brothers at the same time, most of whom are still living, though some have fallen asleep. Then he appeared to James, then to all the apostles, and last of all he appeared to me also, as to one abnormally born.
>
> For I am the least of the apostles and do not even deserve to be called an apostle, because I persecuted the church of God. But by the grace of God I am what I am, and his grace to me was not without effect. No, I worked harder than all of them—yet not I, but the grace of God that was with me. Whether, then, it was I or they, this is what we preach, and this is what you believed. (1 Cor. 15:3–11)

Available to Us

Because of the Resurrection, Jesus can be experienced today as alive and available to us. If he was truly raised and is now alive, he is the Lord over his people and can be known today. And if he can be known today, he is available for the crisis situations in our lives—as he was for those in John's life—and will give us courage and assurance in our trials.

A Foundation for Hope

Because of Jesus' resurrection from the dead, we have a sure foundation for hope that permits us to face this life with courage and to look to a life yet to come with absolute assurance. "Christ has indeed been raised from the dead, the firstfruits of those who have fallen asleep. For since death came through a man, the resurrection of the dead comes also through a man. For as in Adam all die, so in Christ all will be made alive" (1 Cor. 15:20–22).

Well over three hundred verses in the New Testament deal with the Resurrection. Whether it is Easter Sunday or August 9, the proclamation of Jesus' resurrection is Christianity's central tenet of faith. Without it, everything collapses. With it, everything makes sense.

The Triumphal Lamb of God seen in Revelation 5 is the anchor of Christian faith, sign of Christian hope, and stimulus to Christian love. It puts all else into perspective for those who see reality through resurrection faith.

> The worst that man can do is only a prelude to the best that God has to offer. Rebellious humanity thought it had shrieked the final word at Calvary, only to find that God had had the last word on Easter morning. The illusion that death had the ultimate power over life was exposed as false. The Resurrection made death a helpless comma in eternal life and put an exclamation point in every event of daily living. Christ's hope-filled assertion to Martha became the charter of a bold people: "I am the resurrection and the life. He who believes in Me, though he may die, he shall live. And whoever lives and believes in Me shall never die. Do you believe this?" (John 11:25–26, NKJV)[2]

Indeed, do you believe this?

CHAPTER SIX

GOOD SHEPHERD

JOHN 10:11

I am the good shepherd.
The good shepherd lays down
his life for the sheep.

A. S. REITZ ONCE TOLD THE STORY OF VISITING in the home of a friend and seeing a strange biblical motto framed on the wall. The surprising words were these: "The Lamb is my Shepherd." What a foolish confusion of biblical metaphors and texts, he thought to himself. A lamb cannot also be a shepherd!

He moved closer and adjusted his bifocals. Sure enough, the quotation was the familiar "The Lord is my Shepherd" from Psalm 23. He smiled at his initial misreading. But it set his mind to turning over the two metaphors his mistaken reading had mixed. Soon he began to see a fresh insight, though, as he remembered that the New Testament presents Jesus as *both* the Good Shepherd and the Lamb of God.

"The glorious gospel has just been held up before me in a new light," Reitz told his friend. "I am reminded that the apostle John on the Island of Patmos saw a vision which assured him that the resurrected Lamb who shares the throne with God the Father shall guide his people even when they get to heaven. Yes, my friend, I'm glad my glasses were dirty. Misreading that motto has given me a rich blessing, for it could have truthfully read 'The Lamb is my Shepherd.'"

Indeed, the very words of the Apocalypse on this point are emphatic: "For the Lamb at the center of the throne will be their shepherd; he will lead them to springs of living water. And God will wipe away every tear from their eyes" (Rev. 7:17). In the previous chapter, we explored the dual role of Jesus as the Lamb of God—both in his sacrificial role and as the triumphal lamb. In this one, we will look at his related work as our Good Shepherd.

THE FALSE SHEPHERDS

Before telling the parable of the shepherd and his flock, as the New International Version calls it, Jesus tried to warn his hearers against trusting just any and all shepherds who might offer to be their leader. "I tell you the truth, the man who does not enter the sheep pen by the gate, but climbs in by some other way, is a thief and a robber. The man who enters by the gate is the shepherd of his sheep. The watchman opens the gate for him, and the sheep listen to his voice. He calls his own sheep by name and leads them out. When he has brought out all his own, he goes on ahead of them, and his sheep follow him because they know his voice. But they will never follow a stranger; in fact, they will run away from him because they do not recognize a stranger's voice" (John 10:1–5).

A Thief and a Robber

Someone offering to lead the sheep of God's flock may actually be nothing better than "a thief and a robber." Our Lord's original hearers would have been expected to understand this warning as an allusion to either or both of two groups. There had already been false messiahs to appear among the Jews. They had claimed to be God's Anointed and had led their followers to disastrous ends. In the Book of Acts, for example, is Gamaliel's comment: "Some time ago Theudas appeared, claiming to be somebody, and about four hundred men rallied to him. He was killed, all his followers were dispersed, and it all came to nothing. After him, Judas the Galilean appeared in the days of the census and led a band of people in revolt. He too was killed, and all his followers were scattered" (Acts 5:36–37).[1] His original hearers were also being warned against Jesus' opponents who were so actively working against him and trying to draw his growing body of disciples away from their shepherd.

As John wrote his Gospel years afterward, it is a practical certainty that his mind—and the minds of his readers—would apply the thief-and-robber warning to the heretical Christian teachers who were leading people away from orthodox faith in Jesus (see 1 John 2:18–27; 4:1–6).

A Stranger's Voice

The false shepherds would not speak with Jesus' voice—either in content or tone. They would appeal for armed uprisings against Rome, while Jesus' plan was to announce a kingdom that was not dependent upon any particular form of human government. Whether a government was friendly or hostile, the kingdom of God would survive whenever someone's heart was open to heaven's sovereignty. The false shepherds would position themselves for preeminence and power. They would not have Jesus' gentle manner of a servant to all.

Those who knew Jesus would detect the difference in Jesus' message and that of his opponents. They would continue to listen to and follow him, rejecting the call of any "stranger's voice." The gentle yet powerful voice of Jesus would give them stability in the midst of claim and counter-claim among the pseudo-saviors.

Sadly, with the perspective of sixty years behind him when he wrote his Gospel, John could insert this parenthetical note: "Jesus used this figure of speech, but they did not understand what he was telling them" (John 10:6). Other would-be deliverers for the Jewish people had arisen in the interval. Those who had listened to them instead of to Jesus as the "hope of Israel" had perished during Rome's devastating war against that nation which ended with the desecration and destruction of the temple in A.D. 70.

John also knew that false teachers had surfaced in the church—the Gnostic-type teachers whom he had already opposed in his epistles—and had drawn people away from Jesus. Those who had abandoned orthodoxy had listened to the voices of people other than Jesus and destroyed the gospel. They denied the genuine humanity of Jesus and thus denied his suffering death and atonement for our sakes. In his Gospel, John spoke words of truth that the faithful would hear as Jesus' own voice and continue following him—their Lamb-Shepherd.

HE SATISFIES EVERY NEED

The message of this parable is based on the normal daily routine of an Eastern shepherd, a routine which we Westerners can picture correctly only with the greatest of difficulty. Shepherding in that culture—either in antiquity or today—has no similarity to our methods of ranching huge herds of animals. A given shepherd would have a few animals he owned and tended. Not uncommonly, he would move about in company with other shepherds like himself and bed down for the night with some of them for his own security and that of his little flock. It was such a scene, for example, that had an indeterminate number of shepherds (plural) tending their flocks (plural) on a Judean hillside the night Jesus was born. "And there were shepherds living out in the fields nearby, keeping watch over their flocks at night" (Luke 2:8).

The nightly sheepfold was either built in a yard adjacent to a house that used the house itself as one of its walls or erected in the open country as a low circular enclosure. On one side of the pen would be an opening about six feet wide—the only place one could enter without climbing over its low wall.

A Living Gate

That six-foot-wide gate was one of the most interesting features of the structure. The mental picture of a swinging door or rope gate hung from one side of the opening to its opposite is entirely Western. Such a device would have been unknown by and useless to the shepherds of Jesus' time and place. The Palestinian shepherd provided no "gate" to his sheepfold beyond his own body.

As the night came on, the shepherd would stand just inside the opening of his fold and call his sheep. As they came through the opening one by one, he would stop calling only when the last animal was safe inside the shelter. Then, with his shepherd's crooked staff and a rod (or club) beside him, he would lie down in the doorway and sleep with his own body across the opening. The gate to the sheepfold was therefore no ordinary device of wood, iron, or rope. It was a living person. For one of the sheep to wander away or for an intruder to harm one of them, he would first have to pass over the body of the light-sleeping, solicitous shepherd.

What a beautiful description of Christ's role as our Redeemer! In his very person, Jesus is our means into the salvation of the kingdom of heaven. "I tell you the truth," he said, "I am the gate for the sheep. . . . I am the gate; whoever enters through me will be saved. He will come in and go out, and find pasture" (John 10:7, 9).

The messianic background to this metaphor is perhaps found at Psalm 118:19–20: "Open for me the gates of righteousness; I will enter and give thanks to the LORD. This is the gate of the LORD through which the righteous may enter."

This psalm of thanksgiving to Yahweh came to be seen as messianic in its import long before the time of Jesus. Interestingly, all four gospel writers quote from it in their Palm Sunday narratives,[2] and Peter echoed it in his preaching in Acts.[3] It is most natural for Christian readers to interpret the "gate" of this psalm as Jesus, the One by whom his sheep enter into the joys of the kingdom of God.

Savior and Protector

The role Jesus pictures for himself in this parable invites us to see him as both the Savior and Protector of his people. He saves all who will enter the kingdom of God by his person and work at the cross and then proceeds to keep them safe by putting them under his attentive care. The early writer Chrysostom's comment on this in the earliest centuries of the Christian era can hardly be improved: "When he brings us to the Father he calls himself a Door, when he takes care of us, a Shepherd."[4]

The use of this dual imagery impresses us with the truth that Jesus satisfies every need of those who believe in him. What is necessary for us *to be saved?* Jesus. What is necessary for us *to stay saved?* Jesus. To whom, then, do we give all our praise and adoration? We sing "Hosanna" to Jesus and give him all the glory!

We have no desire to admit any thief or robber into God's sheepfold. A thief, after all, is only interested in stealing, killing, and destroying (John 10:10a); he plans only to butcher the sheep. The Good Shepherd, on the other hand, leads gently by going on ahead and calling us to safe and nurturing places; he intends only good for those who follow him (John 10:10b).

FOLLOWING THE GOOD SHEPHERD

Those of us who know Jesus' voice take delight in following him for the simple reason that we trust his leadership. We know his intentions. Therefore his voice has an appeal that none other offers. Going back to verse 5, recall that Jesus said: "But they will never follow a stranger; in fact, they will run away from him because they do not recognize a stranger's voice."

We Recognize His Voice

A man in Australia was arrested and charged with stealing a sheep. But he claimed emphatically that it belonged to him and had been missing for many days. When the case finally went to court, the judge was puzzled about how to decide the matter. He finally decided to have the sheep brought into court. Then he ordered the plaintiff in the case to step outside the courtroom door and call the sheep. The sheep's only response was to raise its head and look startled.

The judge then instructed the defendant in the case to go to the courtyard and call the sheep. When the accused man began to make his distinctive sheep call, the animal bounded for the door. It was obvious to everyone present that he recognized the familiar voice of his real master. "His sheep knows him," said the judge. "Case dismissed!"

Yes, Christ's sheep know him and love the sound of his voice. That is why the Word of God is precious to them. That is why his words have such authority in our lives. That is why obedience is anything but a burdensome thing to those who know Jesus in truth, for he would never call one of his sheep to a place that was not best for them.

He Knows Our Names

And just as a shepherd knows and names his sheep, we are assured in Holy Scripture that the Good Shepherd knows each of us by name. "The Lord knows those who are his" (2 Tim. 2:19).

I heard of a mother who was being asked by a census taker how many children she had. "Well," she began, "there's Harry and John and Martha and . . ." "Never mind giving me their names," the man interrupted. "Just give me the number." An indignant woman stood her ground and said, "They don't have numbers; my children all have names!" That's the nature of our relationship with the Lord Jesus.

The very hairs of your head are numbered! (Matt. 10:30). The Lord Jesus knows you in terms of your peculiarities and special needs. He knows what you need in your diet. He knows how far you can walk without being exhausted. He knows how much heat you can bear. And he knows that you like the sweet grass of his loving nurture and the refreshing water of his Holy Spirit! Why wouldn't you follow such a Good Shepherd!

ULTIMATE LOVE, ULTIMATE SACRIFICE

A "hired hand" shepherd has minimal investment in the welfare of a flock of sheep. They mean nothing more to him than a sum of money at the end of the day or week. So what happens if a fierce destroyer attacks the flock? He takes care of himself! He is not about to risk his life for a day's wages. Only someone whose life and personal identity are invested with the sheep is going to put himself at so great a risk on their account. And that is how much Jesus loves us! For one of us to fail to be saved is nothing less than an affront to his own reason for having come among us in the first place!

Jesus tells us, "I am the good shepherd. The good shepherd lays down his life for the sheep. The hired hand is not the shepherd who owns the sheep. So when he sees the wolf coming, he abandons the sheep and runs away. Then the wolf attacks the flock and scatters it. The man runs away because he is a hired hand and cares nothing for the sheep.

"I am the good shepherd; I know my sheep and my sheep know me—just as the Father knows me and I know the Father—and I lay down my life for the sheep" (John 10:11–15).

Although it would happen only on the rarest of occasions among human shepherds that one of them would die for his sheep, "Jesus gives it as the characteristic thing about Himself as the Good Shepherd."[5] It is the very heart of the gospel that Jesus came among humankind not simply to teach and model the kingdom of heaven but to die so that sinners could enter it on his merit.

While it would be incorrect to understand his statement to mean that God the Father did not love God the Son prior to the Incarnation, this text affirms that some unique degree of the Father's love for the Son is related to the latter's voluntary death for the world. "The reason my Father loves me is that I lay down my life—only to take it up again. No one takes it from me, but I lay it down of my own accord. I have author-ity to lay it down and authority to take it up again. This command I received from my Father" (John 10:17–18). Even in this prediction of his death, however, notice the clear prediction of the Resurrection. He would take up his life again, for the sake of his sheep.

By the process of his death and resurrection, he would unite Jews and Gentiles, males and females, slave and free in one sheepfold. "I have other sheep that are not of this sheep pen. I must bring them also. They too will listen to my voice, and there shall be one flock and one shep-herd," said the Good Shepherd (John 10:16).

THE SHEPHERD THEME

Reading about Jesus' name, Good Shepherd, brings to my mind the shepherd psalm (23). Perhaps a brief look at it is the best way for us to close this study of John 10.[6] While the parable of the shepherd and his flock looks outward from Jesus to his flock, Psalm 23 calls each believer to reflect on the personal significance of being one of the sheep in that blessed sheepfold.

> The LORD is my shepherd, I shall not be in want.
> He makes me lie down in green pastures,
> he leads me beside quiet waters,
> he restores my soul.
> He guides me in paths of righteousness
> for his name's sake.
> Even though I walk
> through the valley of the shadow of death,
> I will fear no evil,
> for you are with me;
> your rod and your staff,
> they comfort me.

You prepare a table before me
    in the presence of my enemies.
You anoint my head with oil;
    my cup overflows.
Surely goodness and love will follow me
    all the days of my life,
and I will dwell in the house of the LORD
    forever.

The incredibly personal nature of this psalm invites us to understand the love of God as it seeks out and blesses individuals. It is neither Israel nor the church that God shepherds; he loves and saves us as persons of value in his eyes. The God who knows our names is known to each of us as "*my* shepherd." So the writer makes the bold claim to God's interest and love without even mentioning the other sheep of the flock. This is not to be interpreted as selfishness. It is simple awareness of how intensely personal the love of God is for his covenant people.

In meeting all the needs of his sheep—green pastures, quiet waters, guidance along the path—God has "for his name's sake." This is not to say that he acts for the sake of some advantage to himself. To the contrary, it means that he does all these things out of loyalty to his nature and promises.

The Good Shepherd will always guide his sheep "in the paths of righteousness." "Indeed, even when I walk *through the darkest valley* (alternative translation, verse 4), whether that be death or some other somber place, I have nothing to fear and I will not fear, because my Shepherd is *with me*, protecting me with His club and guiding me with His staff (verse 4). My security lies not, then, in my environment—whether green pastures and still waters or the darkest valley—but in my Shepherd. In His presence there is neither want (verse 1) nor fear (verse 4)."[7]

Then, when all the experiences of life are finished, what awaits? The sheep in Christ's sheepfold will be escorted into the Father's own house to participate in the great banquet of eternal reward. The journey will be complete. The Good Shepherd will have kept his promise of security for those under his care.

As ten-year-old Bobby faced surgery for the first time, his parents called their minister to come to the hospital and help him calm his fears. After his brief visit with the minister, Bobby appeared to be completely at ease. The boy's doctor couldn't believe what had happened and later asked the preacher what he had said to calm Bobby.

"I first told him that Jesus would take care of him," said the minister, "and then asked him if he remembered Psalm 23. When I began quoting it and he replied that he knew those verses, I asked him to count off its key words on the fingers of his left hand. Beginning with the thumb and moving to his pinky, I told him to let each finger stand for a word in its turn, 'The . . . Lord . . . is . . . my . . . shepherd.'"

"So that explains it!" said the doctor. "I wondered why he kept holding the final fingers of his left hand. He held them tightly all the way to the operating room and right up to the time he went under the anesthesia. He was clinging to *'my shepherd.'*"

May we all do the same in every circumstance of this rocky, winding, treacherous path called life. When we are safely at the banquet table in our Father's house, each of us can thank him for being "my Shepherd."

CHAPTER SEVEN

LORD

PHILIPPIANS 2:10–11

At the name of Jesus every knee should bow,
in heaven and on earth and under the earth,
and every tongue confess that Jesus Christ is Lord.

THE EARLIEST CHRISTIAN CHURCHES WERE communities of praise. Using both the Psalter from the Old Testament and their own original compositions, those believers sang their confessions of faith. Thus we find an exhortation such as this from Paul: "Speak to one another with psalms, hymns and spiritual songs. Sing and make music in your heart to the Lord" (Eph. 5:19; see Col. 3:16).

In terms of their own compositions, several of those early Christian hymns are embedded in the text of our New Testament. The ones that survive to us are probably among the favorite ones of the church, for they would have been chosen both for their appropriateness to a topic and their ability to communicate with readers in a positive way.

For example, here is a beautiful hymn about Christ that is astounding for its breadth and depth of confession: "He appeared in a body, was vindicated by the Spirit, was seen by angels, was preached among the nations, was believed on in the world, was taken up in glory" (1 Tim. 3:16).

In the absence of written Scripture that could be distributed widely and inexpensively, what better way was available for those believers to carry about summaries of their faith? As they worked in the house or field, the lines of this song would course through their minds. As a mother nursed her child, she could sing the words aloud. As a family sat down to a meal, this brief hymn could be the table grace. In any of these circumstances, repeating these brief but profound truths would have had the effect of reinforcing and nurturing faith.[1]

The Power of Music

People of all cultures love music still. And the power of music to shape values and culture can be demonstrated not only from church history but with the frightening memory of militaristic Nazi propaganda set to march time. In modern America and Europe, nothing has done more to legitimate immoral sex and illegal drugs than music. For good or ill, music has power to educate and influence people of all ages and backgrounds.

The New Testament hymn I cherish above all others is the one Paul copied into the text of his epistle to the church at Philippi. To illustrate the point he was making about humility as a cardinal virtue among God's people, he quoted the words of what was likely already a familiar and beloved hymn to Jesus.[2] Whether Paul had composed it himself or was quoting another, we cannot be sure. What we *are* sure of is its enduring power to stir the hearts of believers with its profound affirmations about Jesus Christ.

> Who, being in very nature God,
>   did not consider equality with God something to be
>   grasped,
> but made himself nothing,

taking the very nature of a servant,
being made in human likeness.
And being found in appearance as a man,
he humbled himself
and became obedient to death—even death on a cross!
Therefore God exalted him to the highest place
and gave him the name that is above every name,
that at the name of Jesus every knee should bow,
in heaven and on earth and under the earth,
and every tongue confess that *Jesus Christ is Lord*,
to the glory of God the Father. (Phil. 2:6–11)

Three Affirmations of Jesus

This poem about Jesus makes three principal affirmations. First, it proclaims his deity. The beginning stanza of the hymn expresses his "equality with God" in a pre-fleshly existence. Second, it heralds the drama of incarnation and atonement. Without denying or renouncing his deity, Jesus laid aside the inherent privilege of his standing as God in order to be "made in human likeness." In this act of humility, he remains the model for all his followers. Third, the song confesses "the *name* . . . above every name" that has been bestowed on Jesus in his resurrected and exalted state: "Jesus Christ is *Lord*."

"Jesus Christ is Lord" is a confession not only men but angels in heaven and demons "under the earth" (see Matt. 8:28–34) must acknowledge. He has won the great cosmic victory over Satan, evil, and death. Therefore he has the right to wear the name above all others—*Lord!*

THE SIGNIFICANCE OF "LORD"

The term "lord" (Greek, *kyrios*) fundamentally signifies one who holds a position of authority; one who rules at some level. Another Greek word that is also translated "lord" or "master" is *despotēs*; it sometimes entails overtones of harshness and unpredictability, however. *Kyrios*, by contrast, points to one who has *legitimate* authority. A pretender and usurper might be *despotēs* in relation to his subjects. Only one with the lawful right to rule could be *kyrios*.[3]

In its wide variety of potential settings within Greek culture, *kyrios* would on occasion be simply a polite form of address; it would be the linguistic equivalent of our "sir" or "madam" in English. It could acknowledge someone as a leader in a family or community. It was often used of persons with official position and authority—of an officer in relation to a foot soldier or of an owner to a slave. Occasionally it was even a title given to deity. On this final point, it is particularly important to note the fact that *kyrios* is used to replace the covenant name of God (Hebrew, *Yahweh*) in the overwhelming majority of cases—more than 6,000—in the Greek translation of the Old Testament called the Septuagint.[4]

New Testament usage reflects all these variations of meaning with reference to Jesus. The Samaritan woman at Jacob's well intended nothing more than a respectful address to the man she met there who asked her for a drink of water when she said, "Sir (Greek, *kyrios*), you have nothing to draw with and the well is deep" (John 4:11). The notion of one's status as a leader is contained in this question from Jesus' own lips: "Why do you call me, 'Lord, Lord,' and do not do what I say?" (Luke 6:46). That he was acknowledged as someone with an official status and authority over others is evident in this text written by Paul: "For this very reason, Christ died and returned to life so that he might be the Lord of both the dead and the living" (Rom. 14:9). Yet the status of Jesus as God is clearly affirmed in a verse such as this one: "Thomas said to him, 'My Lord and my God!'" (John 20:28; see Eph. 1:15–23; Rev. 1:5; 19:15–16).

JESUS' DRAMATIC CLAIM

Once when Jesus was teaching in the temple area, he put a challenge to some teachers of the Law of Moses who had been questioning him. He cited a psalm of King David that all of them regarded as messianic in scope. Following the text of Psalm 110 as found in the Septuagint, he quoted: "The LORD says to my Lord . . ." Knowing that this body of biblical interpreters (1) regarded David as the author of this line and (2) believed he was prophesying about the Messiah, Jesus wanted to know how the text could affirm that (3) the Messiah who was destined to come of David's descendants could also be David's "Lord."

This is sometimes called one of the "hard sayings" of Jesus' earthly ministry. Indeed, it does pose a question that Christian interpretation can answer and to which Jewish response falls silent. If—in ancient or modern times—the Jewish rabbis hold that the Messiah is to be identified with the nation of Israel as a political entity, how indeed did David see the Messiah as "Lord"? How could the nation's king see that nation as his sovereign?

On the other hand, suppose the Messiah is a singular person rather than a political body. The statement then has a decidedly different meaning.

> The point made is that David himself distinguished between his earthly, political sovereignty and the higher level of sovereignty assigned to the Messiah. The Messiah is not only "son of David"; he is also, and especially, his Lord. His role is not to restore on earth the Davidic kingdom or the sovereignty of Israel. He does not simply extend the work of David, but comes to establish a wholly different Kingdom, the throne of which is situated at God's right hand. It is thus the question of another kind of fulfillment to the promise than that which contemporary Judaism expected.[5]

From the point of view of Christian interpretation, this is unquestionably a thinly veiled self-declaration. It was an invitation for the scribes of his own time to confess Jesus as the Messiah and to give him their allegiance. He was calling on them to offer the same declaration his own disciples had already made (see Mark 8:27–29). In their failure to confess him as Messiah, they set themselves over against him and his claims. If they rejected the one to whom David had pointed, they could not be part of the fulfillment of what the Holy Spirit had predicted through him. One writer has summarized this confrontation with these words: "This challenge marks the climax of Jesus' encounters with the Jewish religious teachers and leaders. Their failure to respond positively to this challenge marked the point of no return."[6]

Contrary to the claim sometimes made that the later Greek church adopted the term "Lord" for Jesus, it seems clear that writers such as Paul learned rather than created this title for him. The Greek church learned this Aramaic prayer to Jesus from their Jewish predecessors in faith: *"Marana tha!"* Jews and Greeks together prayed, "Come, O Lord!" (see 1 Cor. 16:22).

"Jesus is Lord" became simultaneously the earliest confession and earliest creed of the church.

THE KEY TO PAUL'S THEOLOGY

The most important expression in the writings of Paul—if not in the larger theology of the New Testament—is "in the Lord." The expression signifies that which is done in the presence of, by the authority of, under the power of, and to the glory of Jesus Christ.

Instruction, Faith, and Behavior

What is the source of all instruction, faith, and behavior for the faithful church? "I tell you this, and insist on it *in the Lord,* that you must no longer live as the Gentiles do, in the futility of their thinking" (Eph. 4:17; see 1 Thess. 4:1). All that makes Christians distinctive from others has to do with the Lordship of Jesus.

Strength and Stability

What is the basis of strength and stability in the lives of God's elect? "My brothers, you whom I love and long for, my joy and crown, that is how you should stand firm *in the Lord*, dear friends!" (Phil. 4:1). We find power in the Lordship of Jesus.

Christian Service

What is the motivation for Christian service? "Greet Tryphena and Tryphosa, those women who work hard *in the Lord*. Greet my dear friend Persis, another woman who has worked very hard *in the Lord*" (Rom. 16:12). "Tell Archippus: 'See to it that you complete the work you have received *in the Lord*'" (Col. 4:17). Any ministry that is distinctly Christian is done in the power of the Lordship of Jesus.

Christian Love and Fellowship

What is the ground of Christian love and fellowship in the body of Christ? "Greet Ampliatus, whom I love *in the Lord*" (Rom. 16:8). Athletic teams and humanitarian agencies have a bond in their common goal. The church is bound together by the real and pervasive presence of the Lordship of Jesus throughout its membership.

Hope for the Future

What hope do Christians have for the future? "He will keep you strong to the end, so that you will be blameless *on the day of our Lord Jesus Christ*" (1 Cor. 1:8; see 1 Thess. 5:2). The confidence of believers has nothing to do with their own strength or some nebulous theory of historical progress; it has everything to do with their lives being grounded on the Lordship of Jesus.

What gives the saints of God an ability to smile in the face of death or to be happy in the most difficult of life's circumstances? "Finally, my brothers, rejoice *in the Lord!*" (Phil. 3:1). The ability to write those words while under arrest in Rome has been multiplied in the experiences of countless others who have suffered for the faith. It is not temperament that bestows such a gift, but the power of the Lordship of Jesus.

What is the defining commitment that makes life meaningful to Christians? "Whatever you do, whether in word or deed, do it all *in the name of the Lord Jesus,* giving thanks to God the Father through him" (Col. 3:17; see 1 Cor. 15:58). The church announces to all the world that the path to all that is noble, holy, and eternal is marked by the lordship of Jesus.

The sphere of Christ's Lordship is the church—that community whose identity, nature, and functions are determined by its relationship to him. The church is made up of all those who have been baptized into Christ (Gal. 3:26–27), who continually examine themselves and find renewal in repentance in the body and blood of Christ (1 Cor. 11:28–32), and who proclaim the gospel of Christ to the world (Rom 1:16).

In his life, death, and resurrection, Jesus has shown himself to be the master and sovereign over all things. Thus we must never be content with or dominated by the world's lesser powers. We must, instead, believe, proclaim, and live the truth that *Jesus is Lord.*

THE PERSONAL IMPLICATIONS OF LORDSHIP

Robert Boyd Munger's *My Heart—Christ's Home* is a well-known piece of modern Christian writing that points to the everyday personal implications of honoring Jesus as the Lord of our lives. With apologies to those who know the work and for whom my use may be redundant and also to those who may not know it and for whom my account of Munger's parable may be a diminishment of the original, I know of no better way to make this topic concrete than to borrow from his excellent little piece. It imagines someone becoming a Christian and inviting Jesus to exercise his Lordship in all things.

One evening I invited Jesus Christ into my heart. What an entrance he made! It was not a spectacular, emotional thing, but very real. Something happened at the very center of my life. He came into the darkness of my heart and turned on the light. He built a fire on the hearth and banished the chill. He started music where there had been stillness, and He filled the emptiness with His own loving, wonderful fellowship. I have never regretted opening the door to Christ and I never will.

In the joy of this new relationship I said to Jesus Christ, "Lord, I want this heart of mine to be Yours. I want to have You settle down here and be perfectly at home. Everything I have belongs to You. Let me show You around." [7]

From this beginning, it is imagined that Jesus is invited to enter first one and then another part of a believer's heart. From the study to the dining room to the hall closet, Jesus is taken from one place to the next. The meaning of allowing him to be master and sovereign of the various parts of one's personality and lifestyle gradually unfolds in a powerful way.

The Study

First, imagine inviting Jesus to the study, the library, the intellectual center of your personality. This is an invitation for him to look over the books and magazines you read, the pictures on your walls. In today's setting, it would be a petition for him to see your CD collection, your video-cassette library, and the log for your Internet browser.

Perhaps like the person in Munger's parable, you find yourself feeling uncomfortable as Jesus peruses your mental processes. They may need a good cleaning. You may need to throw away some of the materials you read or cancel your on-line service. Put in their place instead the Bible and music or literature or visual images that will help you think healthier thoughts. Here is the biblical guideline for this room of your heart: "Whatever is true, whatever is noble, whatever is right, whatever is pure, whatever is lovely, whatever is admirable—if anything is excellent or praiseworthy—think about such things" (Phil. 4:8).

The Dining Room

Next visualize asking Jesus into the dining room of your heart—the room of your appetites and desires. And what is its "menu" of favorite dishes? What are the things you seek most eagerly? Would Jesus see items such as money, stocks, and investments? Might he see diplomas and awards or newspaper clippings and photos of you with powerful people?

If things of this sort dominate your daydreams and life goals, you are surely neglecting this counsel from Jesus: "Seek first [God's] kingdom and his righteousness, and all these things will be given to you as well" (Matt. 6:33). He also said: "I have food to eat that you know nothing about. . . . My food is to do the will of him who sent me and to finish his work" (John 4:32, 34). To eat from this menu and to know the delightful taste of seeking and doing the will of God above all else is to experience a satisfaction unlike anything the world can offer.

The Living Room

Then comes the living room in Munger's parable—more likely the family room or den in today's home architecture. It is the comfortable and intimate place of the heart. It is where we go for good fellowship or serious conversation. Jesus likes to meet with us in this room regularly. He will be there early every morning or the last thing at night. He makes his own schedule there flexible for the sake of those he loves! He will go over the day with you and sort out priorities, talk over the tough challenges, and figure out what to do with anything that has gone wrong.

This is an important room in all our hearts. And most of us—at least in the early days of faith—are regular in meeting with Jesus to listen to his words and to offer ours to him in prayer. It is a precious, wonderful time together. Your heart fairly soars as he opens windows of spiritual insight. So many things get sorted out and put right here.

But it is easy to let crowded schedules and distractions eat into your time alone with Jesus in this special place. We begin missing an appointment occasionally. It is never really intentional, mind you. It's just that "urgent matters" crowd out those quiet times alone with Jesus that once were so important.

One thing is certain: He is *always* there and never fails to keep his appointment with you. "I have redeemed you at great cost," you can almost hear him saying. "I value your fellowship. Even if you cannot keep the quiet time for your own sake, do it for mine."

Maybe this is the verse all of us should engrave on the door to this room of our hearts both as a challenge and as a reminder: "I delight in your decrees; I will not neglect your word" (Ps. 119:16). Or perhaps this is what we put on the door to that important room: "May my cry come before you, O LORD; give me understanding according to your word" (Ps. 119:169).

The Workroom

Next Jesus asks to visit the workroom or garage workbench of your heart-home. Well, yes, there is one there. Some tools and equipment may sit rusting. You don't feel that you know much about kingdom work. You don't feel confident about your ability to turn out pieces worthy of him.

"All right. Let me have your hands," he urges. "Now relax in me and let my Spirit work through you. I know that you are unskilled, clumsy, and awkward, but the Holy Spirit is the Master Workman, and if he controls your hands and your heart, he will work through you." So you resolve to trust him. As you carry through with that resolve, he amazes you by beautifying your own character, allowing you to be his instrument for getting someone else through a crisis of faith, or using you to bring some soul out of the darkness of this world into the light of Christ's own presence.

Here is the maxim for this part of your heart-home: "We are God's workmanship, created in Christ Jesus to do good works, which God prepared in advance for us to do" (Eph. 2:10). Your presence in Christ's own workshop of the redeemed and renewed makes you a "work of grace" that testifies to his power. Allowing him to guide you in his gentle, masterful way will make you productive in things you could not have dreamed possible.

The Game Room

Now you start toward the game room with Jesus and feel some hesitation. In fact, you decide to keep back from his holy view some of the activities and buddies that have been the "fun" part of your life. So you keep going to some of those places and getting together with some of those people—until you eventually feel perfectly miserable rather than joyous in such settings. Finally it dawns on you that Jesus must be Lord of all these moments too. So in company with him now, there are new friends, new pleasures, new joys that are wholesome. You laugh and smile. But the things that elicit these responses are holy and healthy things. They are things you can share with Jesus.

The Closet

One day you discover Jesus calling your attention to an out-of-the-way place in your heart. It is a place you avoid. It is something of a secret place where old hurts, old wounds, old pains are stored. It's what Munger calls the hall closet of your life.

"There is a peculiar odor in the house," says Jesus. "Something must be dead around here. It's upstairs. I think it is in the hall closet." You know what's there. That place in your heart contains a few old things you've never been able to show anyone. You didn't want anybody to know about them—and certainly not the Holy Christ. You practically burst into tears at the thought of showing them to him. Yet the thought of keeping anything back from him or the even more fearful thought of losing his fellowship is more than you can bear. So you relent.

He Cleans House

"I'll give you the key," you tell him sadly, "but you will have to open the closet and clean it out. I haven't the strength to do it." And he takes the key and goes inside—ever so gently but thoroughly determined. He begins sorting things out. He throws away the rotten, smelly stuff. He cleans out the once-hidden place of abuse you suffered in childhood or the shame someone inflicted on you long ago or a deep wound from your own foolishness that you thought you could never face. He repaints the room. And he puts in a window that allows fresh breezes to blow through it. What a sense of relief and release you feel to have put that ugly place and all its contents in Jesus' hands!

I Give Him My Home

Finally it comes to you like a bolt from the blue that there is another way to go at this process. So you say, "Lord, is there any chance that you would take over the management of the whole house and operate it for me as you did that closet? Would you take the responsibility to keep my life what it ought to be?" His face lights up, and you hear him reply, "I'd love to! That is what I want to do. You cannot be a victorious Christian on your own strength." Then he pauses and speaks slowly to say, "But I am just a guest. I have no authority to proceed, since the property is not mine."

Munger's work comes to an end with this:

> Dropping to my knees, I said, "Lord, You have been a guest and I have been the host. From now on I am going to be the servant. You are going to be the owner and Master."
>
> Running as fast as I could to the strongbox, I took out the title deed to the house describing its assets and liabilities, location and situation. I eagerly signed the house over to Him alone for time and eternity. "Here," I said, "here it is, all that I

am and have, forever. Now You run the house. I'll just remain with You as a servant and friend."

Things are different since Jesus Christ has settled down and has made His home in my heart.

This is the difference made when one truly yields his or her life to Jesus as Lord and Master.

Will you be honest enough right now to explore and reveal—to yourself, if not to a trusted spiritual confidant—precisely where you are in the process of yielding yourself to your confession? If you are a Christian in your *standing* before God, it is because you have been willing to confess that Jesus is Lord. But many who are Christians in their standing are less than Christian in their *performance*. There is still a great discrepancy between word and deed, name and lifestyle, accepting the free gift of salvation and living the gratitude of a surrendered life.

In a world where "Caesar is Lord and God" was soon to become a loyalty oath throughout the Roman Empire, Paul was teaching his spiritual charges that Jesus alone is Lord (1 Cor. 8:5–6). And some of them would eventually choose to die rather than take the loyalty oath of the empire. With the competing claims of our own time and place, Christians are called to teach, believe, and live the same devotion to Jesus today.

CHAPTER EIGHT

THE WAY

JOHN 14:6

Jesus answered, "I am the way
and the truth and the life.
No one comes to the Father
except through me."

Wʜᴀᴛ ᴡᴏᴜʟᴅ ʏᴏᴜ ᴅᴏ ɪꜰ ʏᴏᴜʀ ʙᴇꜱᴛ ꜰʀɪᴇɴᴅ were about to move away? You'd want a means of contact. Right? Phone number, e-mail, street address, and zip code—you'd want all the information you could get on his or her new home. If that person has really been important to you, you would want to know how to stay in touch until one of you could travel to see the other again. It's only natural. That's how close relationships work.

If you have ever gone through that sort of separation from anyone you love, you have some sense of what was going on in the hearts of Jesus' disciples when he told them: "I will be with you only a little longer. . . . Where I am going, you cannot follow now, but you will follow later" (John 13:33, 36). What would you have done if your best friend not only

89

told you he was leaving but that you couldn't have any details of his new location or follow him there anytime soon?

The disciples were devastated. Jesus sensed, in fact, that they felt like orphans at the news that he was going away and leaving them behind (John 14:18). But out of this crisis of alarm and confusion would come another name for Jesus that reveals still more of his role in the lives of those who put their trust in him.

LOOKING FOR A WAY—JUST ANY WAY

Have you ever thought that Shakespeare's Macbeth was right in concluding that "life is a tale told by an idiot, full of sound and fury, signifying nothing"? Some circumstances so confuse and pain us that we may cry out our own version of that judgment. In such a mood, we cry from the depths for someone to throw light on our path. We plead for someone to lead us out of the fog. We need something or somebody to reassure us that there is a meaning to life.

In the Bible, this character is teenaged Joseph, in prison because of his brothers' jealousy and his owner's wife's lie in a country where he was a foreigner whose God was unknown. It is widowed Ruth, trying to survive a famine with her mother-in-law in a patriarchal society. It is Job, in such pain from a mysterious disease that he cannot bear even the weight of the lightest clothing on his body—and his friends and wife urging him to commit suicide. It is Peter, trying to save his own neck when Jesus is about to die by denying that he knows the carpenter from Nazareth—and hearing a rooster crow in the distance.

In your own life, it may have been the loss of your business, your job, or your parents. It may be the pain that wakes you in the night and causes you to cry for relief. It may be the hopelessness of your marriage. It could be simply your personal sense of worthlessness and shame as a survivor of childhood sexual abuse. It may be some terrible sin you have committed that stands to land you in jail, take away your good name, or strip you of your promising future.

Sometimes life does not appear to make sense. It may seem there's no hope that things will ever be put right again. It may seem there's no good reason to believe that a heart of love beats behind the cold indifference of a vast universe that grinds up huge numbers of people. We may be tempted to say with cynical Solomon:

> I declared that the dead,
>> who had already died,
> are happier than the living,
>> who are still alive.
> But better than both
>> is he who has not yet been,
> who has not seen the evil
>> that is done under the sun. (Eccl. 4:2–3)

When anyone despairs of life in such bitter terms as these, she or he is looking for a reason to go on. He is trying to keep from going down with the *Titanic* of his dream that has struck an iceberg and is sinking hopelessly into the cold, dark waters of failure. She is trying to find an exit from the mess she has made—a way out, just *any* way to go on.

But the way out of life's deep pit of despair is not by grasping just anything that is offered and trying it. The things most commonly offered to people at these melancholy moments typically only make things worse—self-medication, affairs, theft, lies, suicide. The only path that leads from trouble to hope, from despair to triumph is the way of faith—faith in Jesus Christ.

OFFERING *THE* WAY

Let's go back to the original dilemma I posed for you. What about the friend who is moving away? What about your desire to stay in touch? To visit the new place? To have your friend return? Then you hear: "You cannot come." You sense that you are being abandoned. Your heart becomes heavy and troubled.

Then you hear these words of reassurance that seem to contradict what you have just been told: "Do not let your hearts be troubled. Trust in God; trust also in me. In my Father's house are many rooms; if it were not so, I would have told you. I am going there to prepare a place for you. And if I go and prepare a place for you, I will come back and take you to be with me that you also may be where I am. You know the way to the place where I am going" (John 14:1–4).

Are you confused by all this? So were the disciples! Thomas spoke up to admit his confusion: "Lord, we don't know where you are going, so how can we know the way?" (John 14:5). Then comes a response from Jesus that is intended to change everything for Thomas—and for us. We are no longer to think of a way, just *any* way, to make sense of life and to deal with our perplexity. We are invited by Jesus to think now of *the* way—more correctly, *The WAY, the one and only WAY*—to deal with the issues of meaning, place, and function in the often-confusing, sometimes-fatal environment of life on sin-plagued planet Earth. *"Jesus answered, 'I am the way and the truth and the life. No one comes to the Father except through me'"* (John 14:6).

No verse is more dramatic or important in all of Scripture. It invites every troubled heart to find the alternative to despair, shame, and hopelessness—trusting Jesus.

THE MEANING OF LIFE

Many believe that the goal and meaning of human life is to make money and collect "things." So to lose their health is to lose everything. To lose their good name and reputation is to lose everything. To lose their business is to lose everything. To lose their house, car, and bank account is to lose everything. To lose their life is to lose everything. Balderdash!

If the meaning of life is such nonsense, how could Jesus say this: "The man who loves his life will lose it, while the man who hates his life in this world will keep it for eternal life" (John 12:25)? And why would he say: "Do not be afraid of what you are about to suffer. I tell you, the devil will put some of you in prison to test you, and you will suffer persecution for ten days. Be faithful, even to the point of death, and I will give you the crown of life" (Rev. 2:10)?

Too many Christians have fallen for the lie that the purpose of life is to get toys, then die. That will never do. It can only lead to frustration and emptiness. From the standpoint of faith, life is more than competition and toys, retirement and death. In God's presence in heaven, life's meaning is found beyond those things.

The Milton Bradley Company sells a terrible board game called The Game of Life.[1] Children drive around the board in plastic cars to acquire cash and possessions. The bulk of the game is spent waiting for the next "payday" and moving toward the game's ultimate destination: retirement. The one who retires with the most possessions is the winner.

Contrast that with a board game called The New Game of Human Life that was published back in 1790 when George Washington was president. Available now only in historical novelty shops like those found in Colonial Williamsburg, it reflects a very different view of life from the modern game with a similar name. It isn't about the collection of money and stuff. When players land, for example, on spaces like "The Studious Boy" or "The Benevolent Man," they have the right to advance several spaces. When they land on "The Negligent Boy" or "The Drunkard," they lose a turn or go backward several spaces. And the goal of the game is not retirement but "The Immortal Man"—described in the rules as "a model for the close of life which can end only by eternity."

When did we lose this perspective on the meaning of life? Why did we trade it for so selfish a view as the one in the Milton Bradley game? "[If] this is more than just a material world—if, indeed, there is a transcendent purpose to our lives and a unique destiny we are to fill—then we ought to devote our lives to that calling."[2]

On that day when Jesus told his disciples he was leaving, Thomas and the others were saddened by the thought that their relationship with him was about to end. Everything was over! Hope was vanishing! But, no, Thomas. No! Jesus was about to return to his home with the Father. And he would open the way for the rest of us to follow him there.

Jesus' route to his Father's house would be through death and resurrection (see John 12:31–32). As he traveled that way, he would also be securing eternal life for all who trust and follow him. He would go ahead of the rest of us. He would prepare rooms in his Father's mansion. Then he would return to take us where he is. In the meanwhile, we are to view everything that happens to us in light of these facts. A failed business, the death of someone dearly loved, sickness—these are not ultimate tragedies. Only the loss of heaven would be an ultimate tragedy. And heaven has been secured for us by the death and resurrection of Jesus.

It is noteworthy that Jesus gives no details concerning that future state. It is simply being where he is. That, however, is sufficient: "Where Jesus is, 'tis heaven there." This great blessing, the assurance of eternal life with Jesus in his heavenly home, is possible only because Jesus goes away from us through his cross, resurrection, and ascension. If part of the reason for our "troubled hearts" is this loss of dear ones through death, or our disillusionment with this present world, we are called to renew our trust in him and rediscover his gift of peace, in the confidence that he is coming as he promised and that he has prepared a place for all who love him, in the glory that will surely be.[3]

Thomas declared his ignorance of how to follow Jesus to that place, "Lord, we don't know where you are going, so how can we know the way?" And the Lord gave this assurance: *"I am the way."* The way to heaven is not along some path of good works and achievement. The way to heaven is not through education or an esoteric philosophy. The way to heaven is Jesus himself! "Faith in him shatters the barrier of sin and death, and blasts open the road to the eternal life of the kingdom of God. It is 'the road that leads to life' (Matt. 7:14)."[4]

If Thomas had understood what Jesus said in that moment, he would have reversed himself immediately. That is, instead of saying "Jesus, please don't leave us!" he might have said instead, "Then what are you waiting for? Let's get on with this! I'm sorry you will have to die to make it possible, but please don't let our puny confusion and protests keep you from opening the door to heaven!"

The hope for immortality seems to be part of our human nature. We know things are incomplete here. We know our tasks will be unfinished when we die. Life is more than Macbeth's "tale told by an idiot, full of sound and fury, signifying nothing" only if it stands over against eternity to give it meaning. In the birth, death, and resurrection of Jesus, God has spoken on this matter. Life does have meaning. And we can live with purpose and hope in whatever circumstance comes to us here.

Don't miss the *boldness* of Jesus' statement here. He claims not to be *a* way to heaven but *the only way* to God. "No one comes to the Father except through me," he declares. That all the religions of the world are simply alternative paths to God is not a statement to be made by an orthodox Christian. Jesus Christ is not *a* savior; he is *the* Savior, and apart from him there is no promise of eternal life to anyone. "Salvation is found in no one else, for there is no other name under heaven given to men by which we must be saved" (Acts 4:12).

An explorer attempting to travel in and map unfamiliar territory came to a place where he had to cross some very high mountains that were rugged and threatening. Knowing how risky his task would be, he searched for a qualified guide. One man offered his services for a considerable sum of money. "Have you ever traveled through those mountains?" asked the explorer.

"No," the man said, "but I've been part of the way and have been told how to proceed from there."

The cautious explorer said, "I'm sorry, but I will not risk it."

Another person volunteered, and he was also asked, "Have you ever been over those mountains?"

"No, but I've been to the top and looked down on the way that leads where you want to go."

The explorer considered his offer. Then he said, "No, I'm afraid to trust myself to your leading. I want to travel with someone who has been there already."

Finally a man was brought to his camp who said he knew the way. "Sir," he explained, "the place you are going is my home—and I am returning there in three days. I will lead you through the mountain pass and show you my home." The traveler knew immediately that he had found his guide.

The Lord Jesus Christ not only knows the way to heaven but has provided The Way to it in his own person and work. You have found him and can walk with him in the truth and receive his life. It is his free gift to you.

CHAPTER NINE

GREAT HIGH PRIEST

HEBREWS 4:14

*Since we have a great high priest who has gone
through the heavens, Jesus the Son of God,
let us hold firmly to the faith we profess.*

In 1928, BETTY MARTIN WAS A nineteen-year-old debutante in New Orleans. She was engaged to a medical student and getting ready to celebrate Christmas with her family. Then she discovered some pale rose spots on her thighs. The doctor who examined her diagnosed Hansen's disease, better known as leprosy. The physician shouted at her mother, "Get her out of here before she infects the entire city!"

The terror and social shame of the young woman's disease led to a clandestine departure from New Orleans in January of 1929. Only a few members of her family and her fiancé knew she had leprosy and was being sent to a government hospital. The Gillis W. Long Hansen's Disease Center at Carville, Louisiana, was destined to be Betty's home for the next several years.[1]

Other family members and friends were told that Betty was making an extended trip to an out-of-state relative. Her mother and father even went to the trouble of arranging a special mail drop to support their story about her.

When she first arrived at Carville, Betty so feared bringing shame to her family that she gave an assumed name upon admission. Betty Martin, you see, is not her real name. Even though she is ninety years old now and has written two best-selling books about her experiences, she still will not reveal her true identity. Her fiancé remained faithful to her at first, but he broke their engagement on Betty's twenty-first birthday.

Strict public-health laws that were in effect until the sixties dictated the fate of those who had leprosy. They were forbidden to use public rest rooms, ride on public transportation, or to fly over certain states. Husbands and wives were separated. Children born to mothers with Hansen's Disease at the Carville facility were given up for adoption. Detention at Carville was mandatory until a patient tested negative for active leprosy in twelve consecutive tests, spaced at least one month apart.

For those diagnosed with leprosy in the twenties, basic freedoms the rest of us take for granted were denied. Whereas about half a million cases of leprosy are still diagnosed every year, dermatologists treat it successfully and no longer colonize and stigmatize persons with it. How would you like to have been a leper at the start of this century? Or in even more ancient times?

Here is what the Law required ancient Israel to do when infectious leprosy was discovered in the community. Advanced as these instructions were for the time in applying the principle of quarantine to stop the spread of the infection, they are nevertheless cruel in terms of the life of exile and stigma they anticipated. Read the words for yourself: "The person with such an infectious disease must wear torn clothes, let his hair be unkempt, cover the lower part of his face and cry out, 'Unclean! Unclean!' As long as he has the infection he remains unclean. He must live alone; he must live outside the camp" (Lev. 13:45–46).

If you had such a disease, what would you want more than anything else? What would you be willing to give the person who could provide you with a cure—and thereby give your life back? No price would be too great to pay!

All of this may sound like background to discussing The Great Physician as a name for Jesus. But no, I choose to begin from this unlikely sounding background to explore the fact that he is the Great High Priest for those of us who believe in him. Don't forget Betty. We'll come back to her story.

THE FUNCTION OF PRIESTS

There is only one book in the New Testament that develops a theology of Jesus as High Priest of his people. Although such high priestly functions as intercession (John 17:19; Rom. 8:34) and opening the route of access to God (Rom. 5:2; Eph. 2:18; 1 Pet. 3:18) are assigned to him outside the book, only Hebrews offers a fully developed doctrine of his role as High Priest. And the most important verse in the writer's unfolding of this theme comes from the Psalms: "The LORD has sworn and will not change his mind: 'You are a priest forever, in the order of Melchizedek'" (Ps. 110:4; see Heb. 5:6).

"No other Christian writer in the first century drew attention to Psalm 110:4, but in Hebrews there are more references to this verse than to any other biblical passage. The text is quoted directly three times (5:6; 7:17, 21); in addition there are eight allusions to the verse in chapters 5, 6, and 7. Psalm 110:4 supplied the preacher with a biblical basis for the distinctly priestly portrayal of Jesus in Hebrews. The verse is introduced repeatedly to substantiate the argument that Jesus is a heavenly high priest."[2]

Day of Atonement Service

One way to think of a high priest's role is in terms of its contrast with the function of a prophet. Whereas the prophet represented the authoritative voice of God to the people, a priest was the supplicant representative of men before the Lord. Indeed, the high priest "is appointed to represent them in matters related to God, to offer gifts and sacrifices for sins" (Heb. 5:1). The duties of the high priest were focused especially on the sacrificial service of one particular day of the year, the Day of Atonement.

Described in its greatest biblical detail in Leviticus 16, the Day of Atonement was the single annual time of required fasting for Israel. All the other festivals of Judaism were feasts that heard great mirth and laughter. Not so the Day of Atonement. It was a time of recollection and weeping. The nation was called to remember its sinful history. Each Israelite was expected to review his or her own personal frailties. The high priest led this day of public fasting, mourning, and sacrifice.

Duties

Aaron and his successors in the office of high priest had two principal duties on the Day of Atonement. After preparing his own heart and offering a sacrifice for himself, it was his duty (1) to slaughter the sacrifice and (2) to take the sacrificial blood into the Most Holy Place. The outcome of his service was the opening of a path of access to God by blotting out the guilt of sin by means of the blood taken to the inner sanctuary before the Lord.

Jesus as High Priest

It was a beautiful and impressive ceremony. It was a day of mourning for human sin that culminated in the celebration of divine grace.

It is by no means surprising that the unnamed writer of Hebrews should see a picture of Jesus in the office and function of the high priest. "Therefore, since we have a great high priest who has gone through the heavens, Jesus the Son of God, let us hold firmly to the faith we profess. For we do not have a high priest who is unable to sympathize with our weaknesses, but we have one who has been tempted in every way, just as we are—yet was without sin. Let us then approach the throne of grace with confidence, so that we may receive mercy and find grace to help us in our time of need" (Heb. 4:14–16).

By the gift of his own blood at Calvary, Jesus has provided access into God's grace through our faith in him (see Rom. 5:2). Our sin has been blotted out by the sacrificial blood he carried into the heavenly sanctuary. He intercedes on our behalf at the right hand of God the Father at every moment.

THE PROBLEMS WITH PRIESTS

As powerful as it was in its own right and as symbolic as it was of the coming work of Jesus, however, the levitical priestly function begun with Aaron was not without some glaring problems. Those deficiencies make Christ's high priesthood even more impressive. Specifically, those priests were personally sinful, had no better sacrifice than the blood of animals to offer, and could not maintain their office or perform their duties indefinitely because of their mortality.

Sinfulness

"Every high priest is selected from among men. . . . He is able to deal gently with those who are ignorant and are going astray, since he himself is subject to weakness. This is why he has to offer sacrifices for his own sins, as well as for the sins of the people" (Heb. 5:1–3).

The positive thing about the Aaronic high priest's sinfulness was that it not only proved he was "from among men" and "subject to weakness" but also enabled him to "deal gently with those who are ignorant and are going astray." The negative feature about the same fact is that it compromised him as a spiritual leader. Say whatever people may about private life and public life being "totally irrelevant to one another," all of us know better. Professional athlete, musical superstar, television celebrity, president of the United States—whatever titillation or sense of personal superiority we get from their sordid escapades, we know their behaviors weaken the moral fabric necessary to hold a culture together.

Jesus identified with us in our frailty and experienced everything you and I do. The single exception to that claim is sin. Oh, he was tempted. But he maintained the ethical high ground for the sake of his example to the rest of us and for his incredibly more important substitutionary death on our behalf.

Having introduced the topic of leprosy earlier with the promise of returning to Betty Martin's story, let me remind you of a tiny piece of related history you may know. Joseph Damien was a Belgian priest sent to minister to lepers in Hawaii in 1873. He tried to befriend the lonely, frail, and dying people on Molokai. But he preached each Sunday to a mere handful of hearers. After a dozen years of pouring himself into that work, he decided to abandon it and return home. While standing on the pier to board the ship that would take him back to Belgium, he noticed some white spots on his hands. Those spots could mean only one thing: He had contracted leprosy himself. Instead of going home, he returned to the leper colony.

The next Sunday morning he got into his pulpit. Instead of referring in that sermon to "*you* lepers," he spoke of "*we* lepers" and "*our* disease." The news of the missionary's disease flashed around the island like electricity. Hundreds gathered outside his hut. They understood his pain and despair. When Father Damien arrived at his chapel the next Sunday, the small building was filled to overflowing—and was filled every Sunday after that fateful day.

Now the lepers of Molokai knew that Joseph Damien cared about them. There was no longer a question of his detachment or involvement, for he had taken on their flesh. He had taken on their *leprous* flesh and had become one with them. In the same way, we have a God who has identified with us. "Since the children have flesh and blood, he too shared in their humanity so that by his death he might destroy him who holds the power of death—that is, the devil—and free those who all their lives were held in slavery by their fear of death" (Heb. 2:14–15; see 5:7). Jesus took our leprous flesh to wear in order to show us how real heaven's love is for us.

Animal Sacrifices

Another problem with the Aaronic priesthood was the quality of sacrifices. Those priests could offer only animals, but "it is impossible for the blood of bulls and goats to take away sins" (Heb. 10:4). Animals do not have equivalent worth to human souls. Men and women of species *Homo sapiens* are made in the image and likeness of God. Animals may be burden bearers, skin providers, or even food for the part of creation that is closest in likeness to God. Despite the opinions of radical animal-rights activists, Flipper and Coco are not our peers.

The blood of animals offered in sacrifice before the Lord could bring about only an external or ceremonial purification. They could not purge sin's guilt from someone's conscience. "The blood of goats and bulls and the ashes of a heifer sprinkled on those who are ceremonially unclean sanctify them so that they are outwardly clean" (Heb. 9:13). This is not said to depreciate the value of those sacrifices and ceremonies. It is to contrast it with the actual cleansing effected by the blood of Jesus who offered himself for our sins. "How much more, then, will the blood of Christ, who through the eternal Spirit offered himself unblemished to God, cleanse our consciences from acts that lead to death, so that we may serve the living God!" (Heb. 9:14).

Jesus Christ has the power to set a guilty conscience free. "Therefore, brothers, since we have confidence to enter the Most Holy Place by the blood of Jesus, by a new and living way opened for us through the curtain, that is, his body, and since we have a *great* priest over the house of God, let us draw near to God with a sincere heart in full assurance of faith, having our hearts sprinkled to cleanse us from a guilty conscience and having our bodies washed with pure water. Let us hold unswervingly to the hope we profess, for he who promised is faithful" (Heb.10:19–23).

Mortality

The final weakness of the levitical priesthood was its time-bound, space-bound, infected-with-death priests. They had to function in an earthly sanctuary that was never better than a shadowy resemblance of the true heavenly sanctuary. They were forced to labor at altars their enemies could tear down and to function there with tools that broke, that had to be replaced, or that altar-breaking enemies could melt down and use to make images of their idol gods. Even if a given priest should be fortunate enough to serve long in the work of God and could be spared the ravages of an enemy at his altar, he would someday be unable to go to the sanctuary. He would be too feeble to present the gifts and offering to the Lord. He would die. All those who had depended on him would be heartbroken at his disappearance from the holy service. Not so with our Great High Priest!

Jesus is the High Priest forever over his people. He was raised from the dead after his Calvary-gift of himself. He is alive never to die again. The sanctuary where he functions is the authentic and true heavenly sanctuary. And the tools of his ongoing work of intercession before the Father are imperishable and indestructible. "The point of what we are saying is this: We do have such a high priest, who sat down at the right hand of the throne of the Majesty in heaven, and who serves in the sanctuary, the true tabernacle set up by the Lord, not by man. . . . But the ministry Jesus has received is as superior to theirs as the covenant of which he is mediator is superior to the old one, and it is founded on better promises" (Heb. 8:1–2, 6).

THE ORDER OF MELCHIZEDEK

Jesus was called by God to his high priesthood, just as Aaron was (Heb. 5:4–5). But his high priesthood was not of the Levitical order. He was neither a descendant of Aaron nor a member of the tribe of Levi. Of what "order" does he serve? On the basis of his superior qualifications and obedient suffering that made him Savior to all who would obey him (Heb. 5:7–9), Jesus "was designated by God to be high priest in the order of Melchizedek" (Heb. 5:10). Unlike Aaron and his descendants, no one will ever replace him in his office. He is "a priest *forever,* in the order of Melchizedek" (Heb. 5:6).

In his brief appearance in the Old Testament narrative, Melchizedek is a puzzling figure of obvious importance. The writer of Hebrews seizes on this fact to pursue a certain exegetical tradition of his time and make wonderful affirmations about Jesus. Because the figure Melchizedek has no genealogy in the biblical text, he "remains a priest forever" (Heb. 7:1–3). Since Melchizedek blessed Abraham and received a tithe from him, Abraham and the descendants in his loins—Aaron and the tribe of Levi among them—acknowledged his superiority to them (Heb. 7:4–10).

All of this foreshadows the final and perfect high priesthood of Jesus Christ. He is God's high priest not on the basis of Levitical ancestry but "on the basis of the power of an indestructible life" (Heb. 7:16). Thus the author-interpreter says:

> For it is declared:
> "You are a priest forever,
>   in the order of Melchizedek."

> The former regulation is set aside because it was weak and useless (for the law made nothing perfect), and a better hope is introduced, by which we draw near to God.
> And it was not without an oath! Others became priests without any oath, but he became a priest with an oath when God said to him:

> "The Lord has sworn
>   and will not change his mind:
> 'You are a priest forever.'"

> Because of this oath, Jesus has become the guarantee of a better covenant.
> Now there have been many of those priests, since death prevented them from continuing in office; but because Jesus lives forever, he has a permanent priesthood. Therefore he is

able to save completely those who come to God through him, because he always lives to intercede for them.

Such a high priest meets our need—one who is holy, blameless, pure, set apart from sinners, exalted above the heavens. Unlike the other high priests, he does not need to offer sacrifices day after day, first for his own sins, and then for the sins of the people. He sacrificed for their sins once for all when he offered himself. For the law appoints as high priests men who are weak; but the oath, which came after the law, appointed the Son, who has been made perfect forever. (Heb. 7:17–28)

Because Jesus is the conquering Christ who has overcome death, he has a high priesthood that is exclusively his own—for the sake of our salvation.

I began with the story of a nineteen-year-old woman diagnosed with leprosy and sent to an isolated leper's hospital. The man to whom she was engaged broke their engagement on her twenty-first birthday. After all, a healthy man could not waste his life waiting on the unlikely cure of a woman with leprosy. There is more to that story you need to know. Indeed, Betty Martin's story is far more detailed and complex than the few facts I can relate here. But this much you need to know.

Betty did not live the rest of her life alone and unloved because of being jilted by her fiancé. She fell in love with and was loved in return by another patient with leprosy. She and Henry Martin eventually married. Their disease complicated their life together, but they eventually left Carville, fully twenty years after being sent there. They occasionally had to return for treatment, and Betty's disease eventually became active again. They returned to Carville permanently in 1989, and Henry died there in September 1996. Betty is still living as a frail victim of a horrible disease.

My personal story ends better than Betty Martin's story. Jesus took my "leprous flesh," infected with sin, hopeless against the future, and separated from a holy God, onto himself. He came into the human experience to love me as a "fellow patient" in vulnerability and temptation. And he has given me not just a few years of freedom before dying but eternal life with him.

Because he is my Great High Priest in the order of Melchizedek who has overcome the imperfections of the Aaronic priesthood, my sins are forgiven and my future is secure. How wonderful to be loved by someone who would take my disease into himself to save me, who would die from my disease in order to spare me that fate.

And he loves you as fully as he loves me. Therefore, together we may approach the divine throne with boldness to receive the mercy and grace we need in our lives. No one will be turned away who comes there in the holy and compassionate name of Jesus.

CHAPTER TEN

NAZARENE

MATTHEW 2:23

He went and lived in a town called Nazareth.
So was fulfilled what was said through the prophets:
"He will be called a Nazarene."

AMONG THE VARIOUS NAMES AND TITLES GIVEN Jesus in the New Testament documents, one has been distinctly problematic. "So was fulfilled what was said through the prophets: 'He will be called a Nazarene'" (Matt. 2:23).

Which of the prophets was Matthew citing here? No Old Testament text says the Messiah would be from Nazareth. In fact, there is no mention of Nazareth anywhere in the Hebrew Bible. To date no solution to this mystery uniformly satisfies textual scholars.

Some have offered to solve the problem by saying we have a corrupted text. According to their view, Matthew actually said—or meant to say—that Jesus was a "Nazirite." Thus we are supposed to see, in this reading, an application of Judges 13:5 ("You will conceive and give birth to a son. No razor may be used on his head, because the boy

109

is to be a Nazirite, set apart to God from birth, and he will begin the deliverance of Israel from the hands of the Philistines.") to Jesus. We are somehow to understand that Matthew saw Jesus as a "second Samson" who would fight against the enemies of God with the strength of a spiritual Samson.

Other scholars appeal to the Hebrew text of Isaiah 11:1 to say that Matthew may have been making a play on words. "A shoot will come up from the stump of Jesse; from his roots a Branch will bear fruit." This is clearly a messianic text and must somehow apply to Jesus. The suggestion is that the word for "branch" is *nezer* and that Matthew is saying that there is irony in the fact that Jesus was simultaneously from Nazareth and the *nezer* who was to come from King David's lineage.

But I favor a simpler and more straightforward explanation: Nazareth was not a prominent city associated with messianic expectations, and Jesus' appearance from there fulfilled a variety of biblical predictions that the Christ would emerge from humble obscurity and provoke the disdain of those he came to save.

SOMETHING GOOD FROM NAZARETH?

Nazareth wasn't exactly a hick town in the backwater. It was situated along an ancient caravan route from Damascus to Egypt. Sometimes called The Way of the South, this road through Nazareth was the one Joseph had traveled into Egypt after his brothers sold him to a group of traders passing through the region. Three centuries before Jesus, Alexander the Great had marched his legions along the same route.

The fact remains, however, that Nazareth was itself a pretty unspectacular place. It was certainly not a politically important place. It didn't have the status of a Jerusalem or Bethlehem in the biblical text. And recent estimates are that it was a town of only about five hundred people when Jesus lived there.

Thus Jesus grew up not as the cosmopolitan "Jesus the Jerusalemite" and not even as "Jesus the Bethlehemite"—with the Davidic and messianic notions that title might have conjured up—but as *Jesus the Nazarene*. Jesus was such a common name of the time that people wearing it would often be identified by their hometown and/or parentage. What an unpromising introduction and identification to be labeled as a citizen of nondescript little Nazareth.

Viewed with Derision

Andrew, Peter, and Philip had become disciples of Jesus. In his enthusiasm, Philip sought out his friend Nathanael and invited him to join in following Jesus. "We have found the one Moses wrote about in the Law, and about whom the prophets also wrote," he exclaimed. Then, in good form for the time, he identified Jesus to Nathanael by both his hometown and parentage: "[He is] Jesus of Nazareth, the son of Joseph" (John 1:45). You get a glimpse of what it meant to be from Nazareth in Nathanael's reply to his enthusiastic friend: "Nazareth! Can anything good come from there?" (John 1:46).

You can hardly miss the sneer and derision in his words. "When Christians were referred to in Acts as the 'Nazarene sect' (24:5), the expression was meant to hurt. First-century Christian readers of Matthew, who had tasted their share of scorn, would have quickly caught Matthew's point. He is not saying that a particular OT prophet foretold that the Messiah would live in Nazareth; he is saying that the OT prophets foretold that the Messiah would be despised."[1]

Indeed, there are several texts in the Hebrew Bible about the derision God's Anointed One would encounter from those he came to save. The favorite preaching text of the early church contains these lines:

> He grew up before him like a tender shoot,
>   and like a root out of dry ground.
> He had no beauty or majesty to attract us to him,
>   nothing in his appearance that we should desire him.
> He was despised and rejected by men,

111

a man of sorrows, and familiar with suffering.
Like one from whom men hide their faces
    he was despised, and we esteemed him not. . . .
By oppression and judgment he was taken away.
    And who can speak of his descendants?
For he was cut off from the land of the living;
    for the transgression of my people he was stricken.
(Isa. 53:2–3, 8)

Seen with Contempt

In the messianic psalm that begins "My God, my God, why have you forsaken me?" the contempt of many for the Lord's Servant is portrayed with painful realism. As you read them, remember that they describe the Messiah through the eyes of those who see him and are not his own self-description. Sense the heartbreak of rejection anyone would feel who is being seen this way by others as you read these words:

But I am a worm and not a man,
    scorned by men and despised by the people.
All who see me mock me;
    they hurl insults, shaking their heads:
"He trusts in the LORD;
    let the LORD rescue him.
Let him deliver him,
    since he delights in him." (Ps. 22:6–8; see Matt. 27:43)

In his Gospel, Matthew picks up on this theme of Jesus' rejected and impoverished lifestyle. Thus he has Jesus say of himself: "Foxes have holes and birds of the air have nests, but the Son of Man has no place to lay his head" (8:20). He points out that Jesus was castigated as "a glutton and a drunkard, a friend of tax collectors and 'sinners'" (11:19). "Jesus the Messiah, Matthew is telling us, did not introduce his kingdom with outward show or present himself with the pomp of an earthly monarch. In accord with prophecy he came as the despised Servant of the Lord."[2]

Identified with Outcasts

In the Gospels, Jesus attracted such "unsavory characters" to himself that respectable, churchgoing people gave him a hard time about it. "Now the tax collectors and 'sinners' were all gathering around to hear him. But the Pharisees and the teachers of the law muttered, 'This man welcomes sinners and eats with them'" (Luke 15:1–2).

Unfortunately, the world has always had people nobody wanted. Some of them are sick in body and others in mind. Some are "burdens" on their families. Some are not the brightest, and many are not the prettiest or best mannered. Then there are the bad-smelling homeless people. Add to all these the alcoholics, people with AIDS, prisoners, and unwanted elderly people. Then there are the babies somebody decides to rip from the womb because they are inconvenient or embarrassing. And don't forget the people who do the aborting. The number is getting quite large now.

Do you know who would fit best among all these outcasts and unwanted folks? Wouldn't it be someone who was himself an outcast and unwanted? That's the very reason Jesus chose to be identified with Nazareth rather than Jerusalem, New York, or Paris. He is not a trendy-chic savior who hangs out in the best places with the best people. He is like a physician who goes in among his sick patients to help and heal them without thought for his own safety from the infectious agent that is taking lives. "It is not the healthy who need a doctor, but the sick," he once said. "I have not come to call the righteous, but sinners to repentance" (Luke 5:31–32).

Jesus sees himself as the seeker of the lost. Far from avoiding them, he seeks them out. Far from avoiding *us,* he sought *us* out. Anyone who has borne the scorn of being a Nazarene outcast in his own time is not ashamed to claim any among us who will come to him for salvation.

Surely it is part of the total Good News message that Jesus is an equal-opportunity Redeemer!

Somebody's Child

William Kennedy won a Pulitzer Prize for the book *Ironweed*. He later adapted it for the screen, and Jack Nicholson and Meryl Streep played the lead roles. No box-office smash, it was probably too heavy and too theological to be a hit. It is certainly too powerful to be "enjoyed."

In one scene from the movie, the two lead characters stumble across an old woman lying in the snow. She appears to be drunk, as they are. They stand there and debate what to do about her.

"Is she drunk or a bum?" he asks.

"Just a bum," comes the reply. "Been one all her life."

"And before that?"

"She was a whore in Alaska."

"She hasn't been a whore all her life. Before that?"

"I dunno. Just a little kid, I guess."

"Well, a little kid's something. It's not a bum and it's not a whore. It's something. Let's take her in."

So the two drunken vagrants see the old woman through the eyes of grace—even if they are blurry and not-quite-focused eyes. Where others saw only a bum and a whore, grace saw "a little kid" and showed mercy. More than that, she was somebody's daughter—pure and precious on the day of her birth, deserving love she may never have received from family or culture.

From a Christian perspective, couldn't we see such people as persons made in the image of God? No matter how marred the image, it is still there in alcoholics, thieves, liars, and murderers. It's even there still in elder-brother church members and preachers.

But how do those persons believe in themselves enough to allow God to touch them? To take them in? To heal and nurture them back to health? It just might help some of them to know that Jesus was a Nazarene. People had nothing good to say about him. They presumed

the worst. His very background put him under the curse of their contempt. But he had been just "a little kid" once. More than that, he was
the Son of the Father in heaven—regardless of whether others knew or
honored that fact about him.

To All the Despised

Being in junior high can be tough. If you have Dumbo ears, a pug nose,
or a cleft palate, it isn't funny to have people tease you about them—even
though you try to laugh. If you are a girl and taller than every guy in
your class, being called "Big Bird" isn't *your* idea of a good time. Maybe
your skin is a different color or you speak with an accent. You know
what it is to have somebody taunt you, don't you? Or maybe your teeth
are crooked. It isn't that you and your parents don't want to get them
straightened; you just don't have the money. Or maybe . . . It doesn't
matter what the "maybe" is in your life. It lets someone pick on you and
puts you in position to internalize all those negative feelings about yourself. It sets you up for ongoing anxieties and insecurities. Who could
accept *you* with all your flaws?

Forget junior high for a moment, though, and think about life as an
adult—or almost-adult. You are a single parent. You've been in a psychi-
atric hospital. You've had to deal with the memories and aftermath of
childhood sexual abuse. You have served time in prison. You've gone
through the embarrassment of bankruptcy or divorce or abandonment.
And you feel such incredible shame.

Separate Guilt and Shame

I heard Mark Laaser speak at a seminar on sexual abuse that our
Woodmont Hills Counseling Center hosted a few years ago. He made
one of the most dramatic points about shame I've ever heard. I've shared
it with many people since then. Maybe it will help you now. He pointed
out that there is a vast difference between *guilt* and *shame*.

Guilt is what you feel when you do something wrong, something that violates the sense of right and wrong God planted in you. It is a healthy emotion and serves to bring your life back on course. Shame, on the other hand, is a crippling emotion that traps you in cycles of negative thinking and negative actions. Shame so undermines a person that he or she can hardly have a healthy relationship.

Here is the way Laaser summarized his point: "Guilt says you *made* a mistake, while shame says you *are* a mistake." Accept the former when you have to, but never, never swallow the lie of the latter! You are no mistake to the purpose of God to bring many sons and daughters to glory. Your name is on the list of those he loves enough to sacrifice Jesus for their sakes. And Jesus preferred to taste hell on the cross than to live in heaven without you.

Deal with It

Everybody messes up. Everybody fails at some things. Everybody sins. When those failures are exaggerated and one of us crosses the line between appropriate guilt and inappropriate shame, all our perspectives are skewed. We no longer see God, others, or ourselves correctly. God is seen only in terms of his law, his justice, and his judgment; we fail to see him as forgiver of sins. Others are seen as opponents, critics, and hypocrites; we can no longer accept that anyone believes in us, loves us, or wants to give us another chance. And we turn on ourselves. Feeling such terrible shame, we see ourselves as failures, give up on ourselves, and want to die.

Guilt must be met with God's grace and others' love before Satan takes advantage of us to destroy hope! I can't deal with my failures except by the healing love you give me. Otherwise I will either die spiritually or so harden my heart that I may as well be dead. And you can't deal with *your* failures except as you let some of us in to love, affirm, and support you when you are at your lowest.

Confess Your Sins

Whenever you mess up, you need to do three things. First, admit it to whomever you need to. Confess it to God. Go to the person whose confidence you betrayed or whose heart you broke. If it is something so broad and painful that there is no one person to whom you can go, take the matter before the entire believing community. Let the whole church know how heavy your heart is, and let us pray for you and bear some of your burden. "Brothers, if someone is caught in a sin, you who are spiritual should restore him gently. But watch yourself, or you also may be tempted. Carry each other's burdens, and in this way you will fulfill the law of Christ" (Gal. 6:1–2).

Consult a Confidant

Second, when you've confided and confessed your sin, get with just a few of the most mature Christians you know to think through the choices you made that got you into trouble. What made you feel the way you felt? Why did you think the way you thought? Why did you act the way you acted?

Take Pride in Your New Identity

Third, don't accept anybody's "label" for yourself—worthless, hopeless, no good. You are God's child who sinned, who has been forgiven, and who has a future! You are "in process" and "under construction" with God. You have changes to make—changes that God will implement by the power of the Holy Spirit and that might upset some people when they are put into place. But there is no reason for you to believe less about yourself than God affirms for you.

There are, after all, *two* kinds of pride. One is the opposite of humility, and the other is the opposite of shame. The first is not acceptable for Christians, but the latter is necessary. It is what gives rise to a sentiment like this one: "I can do everything through him who gives me strength" (Phil. 4:13).

> Being a Christian is not just a matter of getting something; it's a matter of being someone. A Christian is not simply a person who gets forgiveness, who gets to go to heaven, who gets the Holy Spirit, who gets a new nature. A Christian, in terms of our deepest identity, is a saint, a spiritually born child of God, a divine masterpiece, a child of light, a citizen of heaven. Being born again transformed you into someone who didn't exist before. What you receive as a Christian isn't the point; it's who you are. It's not what you do as a Christian that determines who you are; it's who you are that determines what you do.[3]

Jesus was able to live as a despised Nazarene and to endure the sneers of people because he was secure in his identity. He knew his *true* identity. He knew he was the Son of God. And he knew his relationship with the Father was impossible for anyone to take from him. Now he is able to understand and help you through your uncertainties and insecurities.

Jesus' identification with us was total so that ours with him could be equally complete. Christian, you are somebody's child—God's dear child. And nobody can take your relationship with your Father from you. Rejoice in it. Live positively. Walk with a confident stride.

CHAPTER ELEVEN

MESSIAH / CHRIST

MARK 14:61–62

The high priest asked him,
"Are you the Christ, the Son of the Blessed One?"
"I am," said Jesus. "And you will see the Son of Man
sitting at the right hand of the Mighty One
and coming on the clouds of heaven."

H ANDEL'S MUSICAL MASTERPIECE *THE MESSIAH*, often played at Christmastime, has an interesting history. By most accounts, he had been considered only an average, if not mediocre, musician. He had essentially retired at age fifty-six when a friend gave him a libretto based on the life of Christ. It was, in fact, simply passage after passage after passage of Holy Scripture. It reaches its crescendo in the wonderful heavenly affirmations about Jesus found in the Apocalypse.

> Then I saw a Lamb, looking as if it had been slain, standing in the center of the throne, encircled by the four living creatures and the elders. He had seven horns and seven eyes, which are the seven spirits of God sent out into all the earth. He came and

took the scroll from the right hand of him who sat on the throne. And when he had taken it, the four living creatures and the twenty-four elders fell down before the Lamb. Each one had a harp and they were holding golden bowls full of incense, which are the prayers of the saints. And they sang a new song:

"You are worthy to take the scroll
   and to open its seals,
because you were slain,
   and with your blood you purchased men for God
   from every tribe and language and people and nation.
You have made them to be a kingdom and priests to serve
      our God,
   and they will reign on the earth."

Then I looked and heard the voice of many angels, numbering thousands upon thousands, and ten thousand times ten thousand. They encircled the throne and the living creatures and the elders. In a loud voice they sang:

"Worthy is the Lamb, who was slain,
to receive power and wealth and wisdom and strength
and honor and glory and praise!"

Then I heard every creature in heaven and on earth and under the earth and on the sea, and all that is in them, singing:

"To him who sits on the throne and to the Lamb
be praise and honor and glory and power,
      for ever and ever!"

The four living creatures said, "Amen," and the elders fell down and worshiped. (Rev. 5:6–14)

When he received the text, Handel shut himself in his London apartment for twenty-four days and composed the musical score, complete with orchestration. He became so enthralled with the project that he hardly took time to eat or drink. First performed at a charity Easter event in Dublin in 1742, what he produced over that three-and-one-half-week period has continued to touch the hearts of men and women across the years. You likely know the story that its performance in London so moved the king of England that he stood to his feet, along with the rest of the audience, at the majestic "Hallelujah Chorus." Handel apparently caught a glimpse of the exalted Jesus and communicated it through his music. If only we would focus so intently on the exalted Son of Man that his glory would enrapture us completely!

THE MIGHTY DELIVERER

From the most ancient of times, the notion has been widespread that the powers of evil and darkness would not last forever. God will someday break into human history. He will confound and defeat Satan. He will initiate a new reality among humankind—*the kingdom of heaven*. The person through whom God would act to do all this was Israel's true king, the Messiah.

The word *Messiah* means "anointed." It is an English term transliterated from Hebrew. Translated into Greek, it is *Christos*, from which we get our English word "christen" ("to anoint") and the name-title Christ. In Latin, the equivalent term is *Caesar. Kaiser* is used in German, *Czar* in Russian, and *Shah* in certain Middle Eastern languages. As titles, all these words are closely related. Each refers to someone who has been chosen for and installed in a particular office.

In the Old Testament, two office-holding persons in ancient Israel were explicitly said to be God's specially "anointed" (Hebrew, *māšîah*) servants. The priests were anointed to lead the worship of the nation. And kings were anointed to their office of authority and leadership for the people. There is some evidence (see 1 Kings 19:16) that prophets were at least on certain occasions anointed to their teaching role among the people. Thus some biblical commentaries point to the union of three functions in Jesus of Nazareth—high priest, exalted king, and powerful prophet to his church.

With all this said about priests and prophets, however, the clear emphasis of the Old Testament predictions about the one who would be heaven's unique Messiah is on his kingly rule. Jesus is indeed the prophet who brings divine revelation to completion: "In the past God spoke to our forefathers through the prophets at many times and in various ways, *but in these last days he has spoken to us by his Son,* whom he appointed heir of all things, and through whom he made the universe" (Heb. 1:1–2).

And he is the Great High Priest who offered the one perfect sacrifice that made all previous ones meaningful and any future ones unnecessary: "He did not enter by means of the blood of goats and calves; but *he entered the Most Holy Place once for all by his own blood, having obtained eternal redemption*" (Heb. 9:12). But the role of Messiah is essentially a royal, kingly role. "It cannot seriously be doubted that the dominant motif in the idea of the messiah is the kingly one, and that all other motifs are secondary to it."[1] God's Anointed One is King, Emperor, and Sovereign; both by office and by power conferred on him, he is appointed to a certain special work identified for him.

What came to be known as "the messianic hope" within Judaism is rooted in a host of predictions found in the Hebrew Bible. The Anointed One, whose work would be to redeem the captives and save the lost, would come through the lineage of Shem (Gen. 9:26), Abraham (Gen. 12:3), Isaac (Gen. 21:12), and Jacob/Israel (Gen. 28:14). More particularly still, he was associated from the earliest times with the Tribe of Judah (Gen. 49:10). He would arise from the descendants of Israel's most beloved and spiritual king, King David (2 Sam. 7:16).

Other predictions were commonly associated with the Messiah.

1. He was to be born in Bethlehem (Mic. 5:2).

2. He would exhibit extraordinary character and gifts in service to Yahweh (Isa. 9:6; 11:1–3).

3. He would offer salvation to all nations with a proclamation going forth from Jerusalem (Isa. 2:2–3).

4. He would have a unique Elijah-like messenger to prepare people for his coming (Mal. 3:1–2; 4:3–6).

If these Old Testament anticipations sound familiar, perhaps it is because you know at least the general outline of the life and career of Jesus of Nazareth! He fulfilled every Old Testament prophecy about the Messiah and revealed himself to be Israel's long-awaited deliverer. Yet it cannot be denied that most of Israel—both ancient and modern—has rejected Jesus as the Messiah or Christ of God. How could that be, if he is truly the Anointed One?

THE CONFUSED TITLE

Although *Messiah* beautifully describes the role Jesus was to assume among humankind, there appears to have been considerable reluctance on his part to use the term for himself. It doesn't take unusual intelligence or insight to figure out why that was so: The Jews of his own day had a wrong-headed interpretation of the Messiah and what he would do when he appeared.

Accepted by Jesus

To be sure, Jesus did not deny being the Messiah/Christ and raised no objection when someone applied the title to him. For example, Peter made that watershed confession during his earthly ministry: "[Jesus] asked, 'Who do you say I am?' Simon Peter answered, 'You are the Christ, the Son of the living God.' Jesus replied, 'Blessed are you, Simon son of Jonah, for this was not revealed to you by man, but by my Father in heaven'" (Matt. 16:15–17). Perhaps of even more interest in this regard is his response to Caiaphas, the high priest before whom he stood trial: "Again the high priest asked him, 'Are you the Christ, the Son of the Blessed One?' 'I am,' said Jesus" (Mark 14:61–62).

Not His Primary Claim

Why, then, did Jesus not advertise himself among the Jews as their Messiah? Why was this not his commonest claim among them? "The answer probably lies in the way [*Messiah*] was interpreted by the Jews of His day. They looked to Him to lead their armies against the hated Roman overlord, and to establish such a mighty empire with its capital at Jerusalem, an empire world-wide in its scope, an empire in which God was supreme. Jesus decisively rejected this whole idea. For Him the suggestion that He should establish such an empire was nothing less than a temptation of the devil."[2]

I repeat, Jesus never rejected the title Messiah, or Christ. It was simply that he chose not to make it his primary claim and test among the masses. It had been so grossly misunderstood by so many that it would have hindered his mission. He would have had to spend the majority of his time teaching this way: "I am your Messiah, but let me immediately disclaim your notions of what that means . . ."

Among his inner circle of disciples, he both allowed their use of the title for him and used it of himself. For instance, consider this statement: "I tell you the truth, anyone who gives you a cup of water in my name because you belong to Christ will certainly not lose his reward" (Mark 9:41).

Jesus refused to play into the hands of those who looked for a Christ who would satisfy their trivial expectations. Thus he would not perform a miracle at the behest of Satan to turn stones into bread for himself or supply endless free meals to the huge throngs who followed him early in his ministry. He had a nobler, grander, more spiritual dimension to his own person and goal for all who would choose to follow him.

It is most instructive to notice the way Jesus responded to Peter's confession of him as the Christ. Yes, he told Peter and his fellow apostles that he would build his church on them and their confession of him (Matt. 16:18–20; see Eph. 2:20). Continuing to read from that point, however, one of the apostles tells us what immediately became the focus of Jesus' teaching to that group: "From that time on Jesus began to explain to his disciples that he must go to Jerusalem and suffer many things at the hands of the elders, chief priests and teachers of the law, and that he must be killed and on the third day be raised to life" (Matt. 16:21).

THE CLARIFIED ROLE

The role of Jesus as God's Anointed One meant that he would suffer, die, and rise. His glory and right to reign would not be established with a dazzling campaign against Rome but through humility, suffering, and death!

The rabbis had missed this critical truth about the Christ. They had not, for example, put Isaiah 53 at the center of their expectations about Israel's Messiah. It was an uncomfortable and disturbing passage for them. It tells not of a king but a "servant" who was to be "despised and rejected by men," "pierced for our transgressions," and "numbered with the transgressors." It was too great a paradox for them to understand. Would not the Messiah be a king? Then the servant of Isaiah 53 must be another. Yahweh's Anointed One surely could not suffer, be treated with contempt, and pour out his life. Thus when Jesus appeared as a *lowly* king, they could not receive him.

The rabbis' flawed interpretation was so fixed in their minds that they would reject their Messiah before they would revise their expectations. Shades of the rest of us who have been so enamored of a tradition or some received interpretation that we would miss the blessings of grace before we would admit we had been incomplete in our understanding or imbalanced in our interpretations!

Four devoutly religious women lived in an apartment building directly across the street from a bordello. Their favorite pastime was to watch its front door and to make comments about the people they saw coming and going. As they settled in one night, the first person they saw coming out the front door was a pastor of a big church they didn't attend. "Isn't that disgraceful!" one of them said. "I always said that the people who went to that church were immoral." Ten minutes later, another minister from another denomination walked out the same door. "Heaven help us all!" said the same woman. "People who go to that church have no morals either."

Only a few minutes later, the ladies were chagrined to see their own minister leave the same house through the same front door. There was stunned silence. Then the same woman spoke up again, "There must be someone really sick in there."

Spirit of Prejudice

Prejudice is a hateful spirit that allows us to sit in judgment on all who are different from ourselves and to excuse the inexcusable in those who are our own mirror image. Although racial attitudes are what most of us think about when we hear the word *prejudice,* the longest standing bastion of prejudice is religion.

False Sense of Superiority

Prejudice provides a feeling of superiority by assuming that others either don't care about the truth or aren't very bright. I remember growing up hearing a mean-spirited preacher make some point emphatically and then punctuate it with this: "Anyone who can't see that won't have to worry about it at the Judgment!" What a hateful way to say you are proclaiming the truth.

False Sense of Importance

Prejudice supplies those who foster it a sense of importance by deeming others unworthy. Thus one assumes the worst and assigns bad motives to those against whom she is prejudiced.

False Sense of Belonging

Prejudice promotes the feeling of belonging to an "in" group. Sometimes that group is determined by race or education or culture. Again, however, it has most often been religion—in the former Yugoslavia, Nazi Germany, post-Civil War South, and during the Roman occupation of the Jewish homeland in the first century.

Enemy of Christ

Prejudice thrives on closed-mindedness, rigid personalities, and the fortress syndrome. And Christianity should be the enemy of all these traits. People who follow Christ need to remember that our leader was murdered because he wouldn't cater to closed-minded, intolerant, unyielding leaders who defined acceptability in relation to themselves. In the name of Christ, his followers love people, assume the best about them, and create a community in which all who confess Jesus can belong.

You see, Jesus didn't suffer and die *in spite of* the fact that he was the Messiah but precisely *because he was* God's Christ. It had been there in the predictions all along. The blind guides had simply refused to see it.

These post-resurrection words of Jesus are the most significant of all on this point: "He said to them, 'This is what I told you while I was still with you: Everything must be fulfilled that is written about me in the Law of Moses, the Prophets and the Psalms.'

"Then he opened their minds so they could understand the Scriptures. He told them, 'This is what is written: The Christ will suffer and rise from the dead on the third day, and repentance and forgiveness of sins will be preached in his name to all nations, beginning at Jerusalem. You are witnesses of these things'" (Luke 24:44–48).

To be the Christ of God was anything but the pursuit of grandeur, eminence, and power over others. It was to empty oneself for the sake of others. It was to embrace suffering. It was to be willing to die to save the lost. If that lowly path of submission and ministry was the one both chosen and required for Jesus as the Christ, surely it is the one Christians (Christ-followers) must choose for ourselves.

THE KING AND HIS KINGDOM

As the long-awaited Messiah, Jesus did not initiate a human kingdom of pomp and splendor. He started something radically different from what anyone expected. And many of us have a long way to go yet to understand what it is to participate in his kingly rule. In my tradition, for example, it has been routine to argue that the "kingdom" and "church" are one and the same thing. Thus anyone who is a member of the church is part of the kingdom of God. What a travesty of misunderstanding against Jesus the Messiah!

The church is important in the divine scheme of things. A close relationship exists between the church and the kingdom of God. But they are not one and the same. The church is the scene of kingdom work in the world, but it is altogether possible for one to be a "good church member" and have no part in Christ's kingdom in this world.

The biblical concept of God's "kingdom" doesn't relate well to our Western notion of a territory filled with subjects ruled by royalty. That works well for some people and their notion of the church. Their denomination is the "territory" and "subjects" over whom Jesus reigns— through some often legalistic church "managers" or executive-types whose self-appointed task it is to ride herd on the theology of the group.

Understood biblically, God's kingdom signifies divine sovereignty— the full rule of God in someone's heart and life. By means of Hebrew parallelism, Jesus defined it for us in the Lord's Prayer as that state of affairs which would exist if God's will were "done on earth as it is in heaven."

The kingdom of God broke into human experience in the person and work of Jesus. Thus, well before the establishment of the church, Jesus could say: "If I drive out demons by the finger of God, then *the kingdom of God has come* (Greek, perfect tense) to you" (Luke 11:20). Furthermore, the kingdom of heaven cannot have a "Here it is" or "There it is" address, as a church can exist whenever it assembles; it exists "within you" or "among you" as people experience God's rule (see Luke 17:21).

Immoral, jealous, and otherwise sinful people have filled (and still do fill) offices and functions in churches, but "those who live like this will not inherit the kingdom of God" (Gal. 5:21). Oh, to be added to the church is a wonderful beginning. God adds all who are saved by the blood of Jesus Christ to the church's great fellowship that crosses centuries and boundaries of geography or race. Then comes the real challenge. Will this saved woman allow God to reign over her pride and materialism? Can this redeemed man surrender his selfish ambition, foul temper, and jealousy to the sovereign rule of God?

We human beings seek advantage and position for ourselves. To identify with God's Christ, however, we must—following his lead—die to ourselves, be willing to suffer for the sake of righteousness, and await honor at the Father's hands. Remember? The rabbis missed their Messiah because they could not see him as a sufferer or as an outcast to the Establishment. And so will many of us miss him because the simplicity of following Jesus in the ordinary routine of life rebukes self-fulfillment for the sake of self-denial and denies us advantage over others for the sake of serving them.

Church essentially identifies an assembly of people. In Acts and the New Testament epistles, it is an assembly called together by God. And why has he called this body together? The church is called out of the world in order to pursue the kingdom of heaven. Thus the church seeks to be an outpost of the divine reign in a world of rebels against God. It seems to create an atmosphere where men and women can internalize and live the values of heaven in a world headed for hell. It is the place where Jesus Christ (or King Jesus or Jesus the Messiah) is becoming the all in all of those who have chosen to follow him to the Father.

Because the church is the immediate arena of kingdom-seeking on earth, many passages in the New Testament affirm their close link with each other. But they are not the same. As the church, then, we resist the arrogant claim that we are the kingdom of God. Yet we long for "a rich welcome into the eternal kingdom of our Lord and Savior Jesus Christ" (2 Pet. 1:11). Until that day comes, we continue to pray, "Father, your kingdom come!"

The first performance of Handel's *Messiah* in London was offered as a charitable benefit to raise money for the poor. At that point in the history of England, debtors' prisons still existed. The money garnered by the performance at which the King of England stood for "The Hallelujah Chorus" went toward the release of 142 persons from one of those awful places. How ironic. What a parable of grace!

When God's Messiah presented himself to the world, he was rejected because of the general misunderstanding of his work. How could the Anointed One be a peasant who associated with tax collectors and sinners, who washed feet like a slave, who died like the worst of criminals on a Roman cross? But God the Father recognized and honored Jesus as the true Messiah/Christ. He wept on Friday but stood to applaud on Sunday when the Son's identity was proclaimed by an empty tomb! (see Rom. 1:4). We debtors can now go free from sin's prison!

In your heart is a throne that belongs to King Jesus. To let anything else have that central place is to remain imprisoned and to forfeit your right to experience the kingdom of heaven.

CHAPTER TWELVE

SON OF GOD

MATTHEW 17:5

While he was still speaking, a bright cloud enveloped
them, and a voice from the cloud said, "This is my Son,
whom I love; with him I am well pleased. Listen to him!"

ONE OF THE GREATEST MOMENTS IN THE modern Olympic Games came in 1992. Derek Redmond was the British recordholder in the 400 meters and was representing his country in Barcelona, Spain. With sixty-five thousand fans in the stands and millions more watching on television around the world, he was prepared to run in the 400-meter semifinals.

The starting gun sounded, and Redmond was running with the leaders. Then a hamstring muscle in his right leg ripped. He fell onto the track a full 250 meters from the finish line. A gifted athlete who had already endured several operations on his Achilles tendons was out of the race. It would prove to be his last. Yet he tried to get up and hobble along the track toward the finish line. It was then that something wonderful and touching happened in the stands.

Derek's father, Jim Redmond, had been watching the race from the top row of the Montjuic Olympic Stadium. He came down from his top-row seat, climbed a four-and-one-half-foot concrete slab, and bolted onto the track. "You don't have to do this," Jim told him. "You've got nothing to prove." When his son told him he had to find a way to finish, Jim said, "Well, we've started everything together. We'll finish this together."

A loving, supportive father took his hurt son's arm, drew it around his own shoulder, and the two of them began making their way along the track. The father became, to use his own words, a "human crutch" for the son. They made it to the finish line—to the rhythmic clapping of a huge crowd that was now more interested in Derek's hobble than the winner's 44.5-second victory. Five minutes after he had started—with the official clock turned off and Redmond's race going into the record book as "abandoned"—Derek and Jim crossed the finish line. "It was just fatherly instinct . . . seeing your son in trouble and helping," said Jim Redmond.[1]

Father-son stories like these touch our hearts for what they tell about family bonds, closeness, and love. But there is no father-son story in history that begins to rival the one told in the Bible.

JESUS: THE SON OF GOD

Jesus gave the term "father" a new and intimate meaning in religious contexts. Indeed, he was revealed to be the Son of God in a unique sense. And it quickly became the essential confessional term of early Christianity for Jesus' followers to confess him as the Son of God.

The title "father" had certainly been used in religious contexts before the time of Jesus. Homer, for example, wrote of "Father Zeus," and Alexander the Great was hailed as the "Son of Zeus," in Greek literature. In Greek thought, however, their deities could be called father in the same sense that George Washington is said to be the "father of our country," and famous people could be called their sons in the way that states still cast convention ballots for "favorite-son candidates."

In the Hebrew Bible, Yahweh is designated a "father" to Israel. Yet the use of this title in the Old Testament is neither frequent nor terribly personal. Israel was the "firstborn son" of the Lord (Exod. 4:22). And David could say, "As a father has compassion on his children, so the LORD has compassion on those who fear him" (Ps. 103:13). To say the least, Jesus claimed a relationship with the Covenant God of Israel.

The term "son of God" is not without precedent in Scripture. It appears to be used of Adam in the sense that he owed his existence to the immediate creative work of God (Luke 3:38; see Mal. 2:10; Acts 17:28). It is used in an ethical sense in referring to those who seek and enjoy the covenant favor of the Lord. Thus "sons of God" seems to be a designation for those who sought holiness in the manner of Abel and Seth, whereas those who followed the ways of Cain were called the "daughters of men" (Gen. 6:2). Set apart for God's glory, it was in this sense that Israel was intended to be Yahweh's "firstborn son." But Jesus took the term for himself in a way that was both unique and potentially offensive.

It is not an overstatement of the facts to conclude that "Jesus thought of himself as the Son of God in a unique way, that he was set apart from all other men in that he shared a oneness with God impossible to ordinary men."[2] It is ultimately both a messianic and theological title that claims the supreme place in the divine plan for Jesus. It does not speak so much of the *biology* of his existence—though he was, like Adam, given physical form by the direct creative work of God in his virginal conception—as of his *redemptive office*. It is less a physical than a metaphysical term, less about his miraculous birth than his gracious work of saving sinners. Jesus alone could bear the name of God without reflecting dishonor on it. He alone could be heaven's representative among humankind. Thus he was the Son of God.

When Westerners hear the word *son,* we think of our source of existence and its advantages. But these are not the primary forces of the Asian or Semitic use. To refer to someone as "son of x" was essentially to describe that person's nature. Thus some in Scripture are sons of darkness and others sons of light, one a child of the devil (Acts 13:10) and another a son of encouragement (Acts 4:36). Read the account of Jesus' sinless, miracle-working, redemptive life. What one word best sums up his nature? He is divine. He is God among us!

A Unique Relationship

Jesus is not a created being who owes his origin and existence to God the Father. He has been with God the Father and God the Holy Spirit from eternity past. He is fully equal to them in all the attributes of deity. Under the figure of the Father-Son relationship, we understand nearness and intimacy. Under that same figure, some have mistaken the nature of Jesus as a created being or a mere human being adopted to some purpose by God.

That Jesus claimed a singular and unshared relationship with God as his Father is apparent in two episodes found in the Fourth Gospel. Both show him claiming God as his Father in a way that was regarded as irreverent or blasphemous by the people of his own time.

> So, because Jesus was doing these things on the Sabbath, the Jews persecuted him. Jesus said to them, "My Father is always at his work to this very day, and I, too, am working." For this reason the Jews tried all the harder to kill him; not only was he breaking the Sabbath, but he was even calling God his own Father, making himself equal with God. (John 5:16–18)

> The Jews gathered around [Jesus], saying, "How long will you keep us in suspense? If you are the Christ, tell us plainly."
>
> Jesus answered, "I did tell you, but you do not believe. The miracles I do in *my Father's name* speak for me, but you do not believe because you are not my sheep. My sheep listen to my voice; I know them, and they follow me. I give them eternal life, and they shall never perish; no one can snatch them out of my hand. *My Father*, who has given them to me, is greater than all; no one can snatch them out of *my Father's* hand. *I and the Father are one."*

Again the Jews picked up stones to stone him, but Jesus said to them, "I have shown you many great miracles from the *Father*. For which of these do you stone me?"

"We are not stoning you for any of these," replied the Jews, "but for blasphemy, because you, a mere man, claim to be God." (John 10:24–33)

Jesus' audience that day picked up on the fact that he was not merely claiming to be part of a covenant community that could claim Yahweh as its father. Neither was he simply claiming to be a pious man who lived in devotion to the Lord. His emphatic personal claim to God as "*my* Father" that reached a crescendo in the flat affirmation "I and the Father are *one*" was different from any those people had heard before. To use their own words, they understood him to be guilty of "blasphemy" for making the "claim to be God."

John's View of the Sonship

In the Gospel of John, the sonship of Jesus receives particular emphasis. The claim is never merely that Jesus is pious or numbered among God's children. He has a special and unshared intimacy with God that allows him alone to be called the Son of God. The Greek term John uses to mark this unique relationship is *monogenēs*. Mistakenly translated "only begotten" in the King James Version,[3] the word is used of him four times (1:14, 18; 3:16, 18) and affirms that Jesus has a sonship with God that is qualitatively different from that of all others. It claims that Jesus stands in a relationship to God that no one else shares.

Matthew's View

In Matthew's Gospel, the concept of Jesus' sonship appears often. "All things have been committed to me by my Father. No one knows the Son except the Father, and no one knows the Father except the Son and those to whom the Son chooses to reveal him" (11:27). The term "Son of God" appears not only in the mouths of disciples but of mockers as well. For example, some taunted at his crucifixion and said, "You who are going to destroy the temple and build it in three days, save yourself! Come down from the cross, if you are the Son of God!" (27:40; see 4:3, 6; 26:63). Most significant of all, however, is this confession: "Simon Peter answered, 'You are the Christ, the Son of the living God'" (16:16).

Mark's View

In Mark's Gospel, "Son of God" is the first (1:1) and last (15:39) title used of Jesus. In the only two times he records a heavenly voice, both are affirmations of Jesus' unique sonship. Both contain a Greek adjective (*agapētos*, "beloved") that functions as the equivalent of John's *monogenēs*. At Jesus' baptism, the heavenly voice said, "You are my Son, *whom I love; with you I am well pleased*" (1:11). On the Mount of Transfiguration, that same voice spoke again: "This is my Son, *whom I love*. Listen to him!" (9:7).

Luke's View

In the Gospel of Luke, Gabriel appears to Mary to give her this message: "The Holy Spirit will come upon you, and the power of the Most High will overshadow you. So the holy one to be born will be called the Son of God" (1:35). There is even a confession of his sonship by the demons in Luke. As Jesus was working miracles at Simon Peter's house in Capernaum, "demons came out of many people, shouting, 'You are the Son of God!'" (4:41).

John is consistent with Matthew, Mark, and Luke in their testimonies about Jesus. He is not a good man who aspires to honor God. He is not the most pious of men whom God has blessed. He *is* God in his very essence, actions, and words. And the theme by which they most commonly assert this oneness between the Enthroned God and the Incarnate

God is to represent them as Father and Son. Thus Jesus could say: "I and the Father are one" (John 10:30). Again, "Anyone who has seen me has seen the Father" (John 14:9).

To confess that Jesus Christ is the Son of God is to acknowledge that he bears the divine nature truly and legitimately, that he represents the fullness of God's glory among men, and that he reveals the will of God to us.

HE SENT HIS SON

The Son of God title has a wonderful power to communicate the intimacy and unique position of Jesus. Thought about from another point of view, however, it also speaks of heaven's commitment to our salvation. A parable in Luke tells a story everyone needs to hear.

As Jesus reviewed the history of Yahweh's relationship with Israel, he chose to represent it under what amounts to a Father-Son story. "A man planted a vineyard, rented it to some farmers and went away for a long time. At harvest time he sent a servant to the tenants so they would give him some of the fruit of the vineyard. But the tenants beat him and sent him away empty-handed. He sent another servant, but that one also they beat and treated shamefully and sent away empty-handed. He sent still a third, and they wounded him and threw him out. Then the owner of the vineyard said, 'What shall I do?'" (Luke 20:9–13).

The "vineyard" of this story is God's fertile soil of promises made to Israel about its Redeemer and Messiah. And the "farmers" or "tenants" charged with tending the vineyard stand for the spiritual leaders of the nation. As with every rented vineyard, its owner had the right to expect "fruit"—here the fruit of righteousness—from those who were tending his property. So he sent a series of "servants" (prophets) to those charted with tending his property. One by one over time, those servants were treated with increasing contempt. The owner's final act was to send not another servant but a family member to represent him with the tenants. "I will send my son, whom I love; perhaps they will respect him" (Luke 20:13).

Do you see the critical turning point in the story here? The owner's son has a close and intimate relationship with him ("my son, whom I love") that is without parallel among the previous servants who have represented him. Because of that relationship and because the son had the power to act in his father's name, surely he would receive "respect" from the tenants.

You know where the story is going, don't you? The son is going to be treated worse than any of the servants who have come before him! This was Jesus' prediction of his fate at the hand of his own people. Before rushing to that tragic ending of the story, pause to consider the implications of the Father sending his own Son on such a mission. He must have had high regard for the tenants of his vineyard. Otherwise he would not have gone to such lengths for them. Otherwise he would not have made himself so personally vulnerable at their hands. Otherwise he would have simply evicted or destroyed those farmers. But he sent his own Beloved Son!

This is not simply the story of Israel and Yahweh. It is the story of the Philistines and God, Babylon and the Lord, Egypt and Yahweh. It is the story of all people—ancient and modern. It is America and God. It is religion and the Lord. It is *you* and the Almighty.

You know what the Bible says. You know that the prophets from Moses to John to the person who faithfully teaches you the truth are servants from God. Like John, they bring the call of God for the "fruits of repentance" to us. But we resist. We balk at the right of anyone to make a demand on us—even (perhaps *especially*) in the name of God. On our best days, we discover that we cannot bring what the Lord is due from us. Our best just isn't that good. Our righteousness is tattered and pitiful compared to the perfect holiness of our God.

Someone protests, "But at least you and I weren't the murderers of Jesus!" Really? I see myself as guilty of his blood as either Pilate or Caiaphas. It wasn't just the sins of Jesus' contemporaries that nailed him to a Roman cross outside Jerusalem. He died for my sins as well as theirs. Therefore, I see myself as responsible for his death as they were. The accident of their temporal and spatial nearness to the event over mine is merely that—an accident of history. My moral-spiritual responsibility is fully as great as theirs.

Follow the story line closely. The final person sent into the owner's vineyard was not a servant hoping to become a son by executing some super-perilous mission. His sonship was prior to and independent of his mission. Indeed, it was because he was the owner's son, representative, and heir that he had an expectation of its success. But because he was the heir, he was treated more horribly than the servants who had gone before him. "But when the tenants saw him, they talked the matter over. 'This is the heir,' they said. 'Let's kill him, and the inheritance will be ours.' So they threw him out of the vineyard and killed him" (Luke 20:14–15).

RECEIVING THE SON

At the conclusion of his parable of the wicked tenants, Jesus summed up its lesson by citing Psalm 118:22 and called his hearers to reflect on its message. "Jesus looked directly at them and asked, 'Then what is the meaning of that which is written: "The stone the builders rejected has become the capstone"? Everyone who falls on that stone will be broken to pieces, but he on whom it falls will be crushed'" (Luke 20:17–18).

Jesus remains the centerpiece of heaven's redemptive work. Whether men accept him or reject him does not change his nature or role. There is no replacing him in the plan of God. Following his rejection and death at the hands of his contemporaries, God vindicated him by raising him up and exalting him to the highest place. Thus Paul would later write that Jesus "was declared with power to be the Son of God by his resurrection from the dead" (Rom. 1:4). If people of later generations should reject him too, the Son will be their judge at the final day (Acts 17:31).

Anyone who rejects and opposes the capstone in God's plan will only be crushed by it. Though men reject him, heaven has authenticated him as the one and only Savior. There is no replacing this chosen and matchless stone, the Beloved Son of God.

139

But what of those who receive him? What of those who make the ancient confession that they believe in Jesus as the Son of God? The following verses from the prologue to John's Gospel sound as if they were written as commentary on Jesus' parable of the wicked tenants: "He came to that which was his own, but his own did not receive him. Yet to all who received him, to those who believed in his name, he gave the right to become children of God—children born not of natural descent, nor of human decision or a husband's will, but born of God" (John 1:11–13).

Jesus is the Son of God in a sense that none other can be. He shares the divine essence. In his very nature, he is God from eternity past through eternity future. Yet he has made it possible for us to participate in his status as children of God. We cannot share in the divine essence, but we can experience divine transformation and personal regeneration. We can be "co-heirs with Christ" to all the Father's spiritual resources (Rom. 8:17).

Here is what Paul wrote on this point: "When the time had fully come, God sent his Son, born of a woman, born under law, to redeem those under law, that we might receive the full rights of sons. Because you are sons, God sent the Spirit of his Son into our hearts, the Spirit who calls out, 'Abba, Father.' So you are no longer a slave, but a son; and since you are a son, God has made you also an heir" (Gal. 4:4–7).

Abba

Abba is an Aramaic word used for one's father within the family circle. In the Talmud, for example, we are told: "When a child experiences the taste of wheat (i.e., when he or she is weaned), it learns to say *abba* (i.e., daddy) and *imma* (i.e., mommy)."[4] Even as the children matured and became adults, this term of intimacy and special respect would continue to be used within a close family. Although there is not a single case known to us of God being addressed as *abba* in Jewish prayer literature, it is the way we are taught to address him. What was thought too personal and too familiar by the rabbis is commonplace for Christians.

140

Why? Because Jesus prayed to his Father as *abba* and we share in his son-ship to God. At Gethsemane, Mark uses the Aramaic term in his Greek account of Christ's prayer: *"Abba*, Father, everything is possible for you. Take this cup from me. Yet not what I will, but what you will" (Mark 14:36).

Abba is probably the term Jesus always used for prayer in his native Aramaic. At the least, we know he called God "Father"—if not *Abba*—in every one of his prayers recorded in the Gospels. The single exception is his cry from the cross, "My God, my God, why have you forsaken me?" (Matt 27:46). In that exceptional case, he was quoting Psalm 22 and used the form of address already fixed in that text.

Jesus didn't learn this intimate language for prayer from others. It was his own personal way of talking with God that we imitate with his blessing. Such language "expresses the heart of Jesus' relationship to God. He spoke to God as a child to its father; confidently and securely, and yet at the same time reverently and obediently."[5]

Now Jesus invites us to pray: "Our Father in heaven . . ." (Matt. 6:9–13). But how can that be? Can any human being partake of the nature of God and be a son of God as Jesus was? Absolutely not. Jesus is the Son of God in his own essence, yet we may become children of God by grace. Jesus is the Son of God by nature; we may be his sons by adoption. Jesus is the Son of God by right of holiness; we are sons of God by virtue of regeneration in which his holiness is credited to us.

YOUR PERSONAL INTIMACY WITH GOD

Because of the merciful love of Jesus that invites us to share his intimacy with all things divine, we have a status with God that fairly begs to be shouted from the rooftops. "How great is the love the Father has lavished on us, that we should be called children of God!" declares John. "And that is what we are!" (1 John 3:1).

And read what Paul wrote on this point: "How blessed is God! And what a blessing he is! He's the Father of our Master, Jesus Christ, and takes us to the high places of blessing in him. Long before he laid down earth's foundations, he had us in mind, had settled on us as the focus of his love, to be made whole and holy by his love. Long, long ago he decided to adopt us into his family through Jesus Christ. (What pleasure he took in planning this!) He wanted us to enter into the celebration of his lavish gift-giving by the hand of his beloved Son" (Eph. 1:3–6, *The Message*).

Ceremony of Adoption

In the Roman world of Jesus' time, a young man reaching his legal age for manhood went through a public ceremony. It was customary for his father to take him into the city forum. There, from a public platform, he would announce to the citizens of that city: "This is my son. He has come of age. Today he inherits my name, my property, and my social position among you." Then he would take off the customary *toga praetexta* of a Roman boy and put on him the *toga virilis*, the coat of manhood. This act of public announcement and claiming of one's son was called "adoption."

When early Christians emerged from their baptism, it was customary to place a white toga on them. Modern readers would immediately and naturally see the symbolism of a *robe of purity* in reading those accounts. One who had been baptized into Christ stood before God in his righteousness. But we may have missed the dual symbolism of the *robe of adoption*.

As God's children through Christ, we have a standing with him that neither Greek philosophers nor Jewish rabbis dared to envision. Jesus' offensiveness to his contemporaries in calling God *"my* Father" and teaching his disciples to pray *"our* Father" should be incredibly encouraging to us in our spiritual frailty. Yet some of us seem not to appreciate the high standing we have been given.

If you are old enough to remember the presidency of John F. Kennedy or if you have read anything about his White House years, you likely have those pictures of his two children running free in the halls of power burned into your mind. Whatever your political affiliation or attitude toward Kennedy, you have to admit that a nation's heart was captured by the sight of Caroline and John-John rushing past schedulers, cabinet members, and security guards to plop into their daddy's lap. Children have access to their fathers that doesn't have to be mediated through underlings! Do you realize that is your relationship to God in Christ Jesus?

YOUR *ABBA* POSSIBILITIES

I don't mean to be irreverent when I suggest that the God of the cosmos wants us to think of him in terms of his *Abba*-ness to us. He wants to be thought of less as Creator, Ruler, and Sovereign—though he is all that and much more—than as a daddy who is trying to help his kids grow up. Yes, we must preserve the mystery and majesty surrounding our human conceptions of God. But we must somehow balance reverence with intimacy, respect with nearness, awe with approachability.

No one ever had an earthly father who deserved more respect and admiration than mine. I was and continue to be in awe of him. He was and is my ideal of Christian manhood. But I never once began a conversation with him saying, "Father, it is . . ." All my conversations started, "Daddy." And in pressing this point in relation to God, I'm not even suggesting that we now begin our prayers with "Our Dad who is in heaven . . ." (I don't know of anything wrong with that, mind you.) The point is that I want to know God so personally through his ideal and perfect Son that I can sense his love as Jesus did. So here are some things Scripture says about God's attitude toward us that might help you feel nearer to him or even help you overcome images of a less-than-ideal earthly father you might have experienced.

Your Abba Has Accepted and Adopted You

I dare say that you know the terms "unexpected pregnancy" and "unwanted child," don't you? Neither term fits you! "In love [God the Father] predestined us to be adopted as his sons through Jesus Christ, in accordance with his pleasure and will" (Eph. 1:4–5). You are a planned and purposed, chosen and adopted child. It isn't that God did something that unexpectedly made him have to deal with you. He acted altogether deliberately to claim you as his own. You are in his family because he wants you there and has pursued you to be his own.

The human adoption process requires a thoughtful decision followed by a multipaged application. It requires home visits and inquiries into two people's work history and financial status. It's harder than getting babies the way Myra and I got our three. If we'd had to prove only our financial worthiness to have a child, we'd never have gotten Michelle when we did. I admit to admiring those adults who are willing to open up their medical histories, family trees, psyches, and relationships for strangers to probe in order to receive a child by adoption. They go through a long, grueling ordeal to prove their worthiness to love a child. Yet no one has ever gone the lengths God has to make you his child. If you sense rejection and abandonment in other settings and relationships, you are secure in this one.

Your Abba Is Proud of You

Is that a shocking notion to your mind? Isn't the central theme of biblical theology how bad and sinful we humans are in God's eyes? Absolutely not! The dominant and defining truth of biblical theology is God's grace, not human wickedness. And while it is important to realize how sinful we are, it is far more important to accept how loving and forgiving God is. Adoration and worship do not develop out of fear but from gratitude.

If heaven had a den with a family picture table in it like we do at our house, your Father would put your picture on it. If he had a refrigerator, he would have something stuck to its door to remind him of you. I know he would, for that is how parents are about the children they love. I am so proud of my three children. Got a minute? I'll tell you something special and wonderful about each one of them in turn. Are they perfect?

Haven't they ever messed up? Didn't I ever have to discipline or even punish them? The blotches on my kids' records don't mean a thing to me. I'm proud of them. I love them unconditionally. I will never be ashamed to claim them.

Here's a verse you may have missed in reading your Bible: "Jesus is not ashamed to call them brothers" (Heb. 2:11). Who's the "them" of this verse? The rest of the children God has taken into his family. Do you know what Jesus will say to his Father on the Last Great Day? He will take his place with all of us who have been touched by his blood and say, "Here am I, and the children God has given me" (Heb. 2:13). It sounds like a big brother who has just fought off the neighborhood bully and made it home to his dad's house. "Dad, I'm home," he says, "along with the rest of the kids you told me to look after!" If Jesus isn't ashamed to call you his sister or brother, his *Abba* must be proud of you too.

Your Abba Is Big Enough to Take Care of You

The only reason I ever thought it would be desirable to "freeze" our children at a given age was not some cute lisp or expression or trick in their repertoire—for I can honestly say that I have enjoyed each of them more and more as they have grown and matured. I simply hated for them to grow up and find out that I wasn't able to do everything they needed or wanted, that I wouldn't always be able to keep them safe or fix what went wrong.

For instance, when Michelle was five years old, she came to me one night sobbing her heart out. When I could calm her enough to find out what had happened, she explained to me that Michael's head had fallen off! Michael was her favorite doll, and I still believe she learned some of her excellent mothering skills on him. But he was one of those "basic" dolls that Fisher-Price would hardly consider making today. He was just plastic head, feet, and hands on a cloth body. That day Michael's head had come loose and fallen off, and my baby was devastated. So I constructed a scenario of a hospital that could repair baby dolls. With her and her mother as nurse assistants, I surgically reattached Michael's head with a loop of wire far stronger than the string that originally held it in place. Last Sunday night, my daughter's daughter came to our house and brought a doll with her. Do you want to guess his name? When Michelle came in the house with her baby hugging Michael, she asked, "Do you remember this doll?" Do I remember? It may have been the biggest day of my life with my own daughter. She thought her daddy could do anything! And I distinctly remember thinking that night how I dreaded the day when things would happen in my little girl's life that I wouldn't have a clue how to tackle. With God as your Father, you have the security of knowing that he is never at a loss to know how to help his sons and daughters through their great life challenges. "In [Christ] and through faith in him we may approach God with freedom and confidence" (Eph. 3:12). "God is faithful; he will not let you be tempted beyond what you can bear" (1 Cor. 10:13). "[Nothing] in all creation, will be able to separate us from the love of God that is in Christ Jesus our Lord" (Rom. 8:39).

Your Abba Challenges You to Grow

An eleven-year-old girl who had been seriously injured in a car wreck and whose crushed left hip had been rebuilt by doctors was frustrated with her physical therapy. One day when her father was trying to encourage her through some painful exercises, she fell into his arms and began crying uncontrollably. "Daddy, don't you love me just the way I am?" she asked. Sensing how she felt, he held her close and answered through his own tears to say, "Yes, sweetheart, I love you just the way you are. But I love you too much to let you stay that way."

God loves you just the way you are—flaws, handicaps, injuries, repairs, open wounds. He loves you even though you are struggling with sin. And there is nothing you can do to make him love you more than he already does. He loves you because you are his child and not because you are perfect, won't sin anymore, or will serve him in some spectacular way. He has forgiven you and adopted you as his child on the basis of the saving work of his singular, incomparable, beloved Son Jesus. But he loves you too much to let you remain as you are. In all your weakness, difficulties, and sinfulness, he is working to change your personality and character to be more like Jesus.

A New Testament writer once compared the Christian life to a "race marked out for us" (Heb. 12:1–3). The word picture he paints invites us to envision a stadium whose stands are filled with a "great cloud of witnesses"—veterans of the race we are now running. More important still, he urges all of us running the Christian race to "fix our eyes on Jesus"— the One who has finished the race already and who has been crowned and enthroned for his victory.

Jesus "went down" during his race. He sprawled on the track, appeared to the medics to be dead, and was put in the morgue on Friday afternoon. By Sunday morning, his Father had worked his way out of the stands and into the tomb with Jesus. He draped his Son's arm around his own neck, raised him up from that grave, and walked him across his personal finish line. By that powerful act, God identified himself with Jesus and declared him to be the Son of God (see Rom. 1:4).

Are you getting weary in your race? Does the finish line appear too far away? Are you about to lose heart for the run? Keep your eyes on Jesus! Know that you have the deep reserves of the Indwelling Spirit for your stretch run! And if you should go down on the track from exhaustion or injury, your Father will come out of the stands and carry you by his strength across your personal finish line. And you will stand there with Jesus in glorious and eternal triumph!

Derek Redmond crossed the finish line in Barcelona under his father's power, not his own. Jesus triumphed in his redemptive work because the Father raised him from the dead. And that's my assurance about the race we are running. No one who will lean on the Father's everlasting arms will fail to finish the race!

For the sake of his incomparable and beloved Son, God is completing in us the work he started in him. On the basis of Christ's triumph, then, be confident of your own. Don't look down at your tired feet. Look upward to the Son in his glory. And rejoice in this biblical text about our shared sonship with Jesus:

> In bringing many sons to glory, it was fitting that God, for whom and through whom everything exists, should make the author of their salvation perfect through suffering. Both the one who makes men holy and those who are made holy are of the same family. So Jesus is not ashamed to call them brothers. He says,
>
> "I will declare your name to my brothers;
> > in the presence of the congregation I will sing your
> > praises."
>
> And again,
>
> "I will put my trust in him."
>
> And again he says,
>
> "Here am I, and the children God has given me." (Heb. 2:10–13)

CHAPTER THIRTEEN

SON OF MAN

LUKE 9:22

*The Son of Man must suffer many things
and be rejected by the elders, chief priests
and teachers of the law, and he must be killed
and on the third day be raised to life.*

IT IS A PLOT THAT HAS BEEN USED IN BOOKS and movies for centuries. The hero has taken it upon himself to anonymously defend and serve his nation, his tribe, or a wronged person. He proves himself brave and faithful. Word of his goodness spreads, and people begin to admire him for his exploits. Then he is cornered and about to be found out.

The villain of the story has key players in the town square or in his court. "Unless The Masked Avenger (or whatever his identity in the story) makes himself known, I will kill the lot of you!" he sneers. So our hero's nobility moves him to speak from the edge of the crowd and say, "*I am The Masked Avenger.*" But no sooner does he speak than someone on the other side of the group says, "*I am The Masked Avenger.*" Then a third speaks, a fourth, and fifth. The villain is crestfallen then as everyone in the crowd is shouting, *"I am the Masked Avenger."* Thus rallied and united, the group unites, rises up against the evil predator, and things are set right. Fade to black . . .

This compelling theme of solidarity is the approach I want to offer you for understanding, embracing, and appreciating one of the most complex and puzzling of the titles used by Jesus. What did he mean to communicate to us when he constantly referred to himself as the Son of Man?

JESUS' DESIGNATION OF CHOICE

The expression "Son of Man" occurs approximately eighty times in the four Gospels. It is always on the lips of Jesus.[1] Approximately seventy times in the synoptics—Matthew, Mark, and Luke—and about ten more in John, he insists on making it his preferred self-designation. The simple fact that Jesus calls himself Son of Man more times than any other of the rich names to which he was entitled practically demands that we try to find why.

Although the term has multifaceted significance, we begin with a text in which it appears as a rebuke and corrective. From this beginning, we will work outward to collect biblical information that illuminates the title Son of Man.

When Peter and the other apostles had been with Jesus long enough to know something of his character, works, and teaching, Jesus put the all-important question to them: "Who do you say I am?" In one account of the exchange, Peter's immediate reply was this: "The Christ of God" (Luke 9:20). In another record of the same event, Peter's slightly fuller confession takes this form: "You are the Christ, the Son of the Living God" (Matt. 16:16). Thus two titles—"Christ" and "Son of the Living God"—are attributed to Jesus. When we confess him as the long-awaited Jewish Messiah, we confess his deity.

It is most important for our purposes here to closely examine Jesus' reply to that confession.

Jesus strictly warned them not to tell this to anyone. And he said, "The *Son of Man* must suffer many things and be rejected by the elders, chief priests and teachers of the law, and he must be killed and on the third day be raised to life."

Then he said to them all: "If anyone would come after me, he must deny himself and take up his cross daily and follow me. For whoever wants to save his life will lose it, but whoever loses his life for me will save it. What good is it for a man to gain the whole world, and yet lose or forfeit his very self? If anyone is ashamed of me and my words, the *Son of Man* will be ashamed of him when he comes in his glory and in the glory of the Father and of the holy angels." (Luke 9:21–26)

The importance I attach to the title Son of Man is highlighted brilliantly in this single text. Go back for a moment to the story line that was sketched at the beginning of the defender-hero, oppressor-villain, and hapless-grateful crowd. It is an account of identification and solidarity. The one man identifies with the masses and acts on behalf of the entire group. In turn, the masses express such solidarity with the one man that they refuse to see themselves any further except in relation to him. He took their slights, injustices, and mistreatment onto himself; they then stand in grateful association and fraternity with him, willing even to put themselves at risk for the sake of the one who has already been at peril for their sakes.

The shared hope of both the hero and those to whose defense he has come is that they will eventually stand together in triumph before the story ends. The reason such a story is so engaging is that it captures in fictional form the inspiring majesty of what Jesus has done for us as the Son of Man.

An Early Interpretation: Weakness

Do you recall the brief discussion earlier on the Semitic, or Hebrew, expression "son of x"? As we said, it is sometimes quite different from our Western (Greek) use of the term. Because Westerners most often use a predicate such as "John is the *son of* . . ." to give information on a person's origin, we would be saying that John would not have existed except for the one who fathered him or that John owes his existence to the prior life of another. As Easterners sometimes use the same expression, it describes a person's nature. That is why we get expressions like "sons of light" or "Son of Encouragement" in our Bibles. They are descriptive terms about someone's character and lifestyle, not accounts of his or her origin.

This important information about the Semitic "son of . . ." was introduced previously in connection with Son of God as a title for Jesus. God the Father and God the Son are both eternal, self-existing, and fully equal in their persons. Neither owes his origin to the other. Neither brought the other into existence or conferred status on the other. Neither is superior to or greater than the other. Whatever God the Father is, God the Son is also. Any glory or praise or worship the one is entitled to receive, the other deserves as well. To say, then, that Jesus is the Son of God is to say that his nature is one and the same with the Father and the Holy Spirit, that he is divine in his very essence. Father, Son, and Spirit are united by virtue of their shared deity.

Completely God and Man

So what does it mean to say of Jesus that he is not only the Son of God but also the Son of Man? It announces the staggering mystery of the Incarnation—God coming among us in flesh-and-blood form—and affirms in still another way that God has become one with humankind so that we may become one with God. In Jesus Christ, God identified with our frailty and weakness so that we could ultimately stand in solidarity with him in glory. Jesus, you, and I are united by virtue of our shared humanity. "There is one God and one mediator between God and men, the man Christ Jesus, who gave himself as a ransom for all men—the testimony given in its proper time" (1 Tim. 2:5–6).

Two of my all-time favorite quotations about the meaning of the Incarnation capture the essence of what I am trying to communicate here.

> There is nothing that might be called otherworldly about this ministry of Jesus. He scandalized the religious leaders of his day, the prim and proper ones, because he consorted with the social and religious pariahs of his day: the tax collectors who were despised and hated because they collaborated with the Romans. His friends were the ladies of easy virtue who went about with uncovered heads, who made public spectacles of themselves at parties, clutching the feet of strange young men and weeping over them and wiping them with their long hair. . . . Such were his friends, the ones who were looked down upon. No wonder one of the favorite titles for Jesus today, which captivates so many, is calling him *the man for others.*[2]

And the second: "The Son of God became man to enable men to become the sons of God."[3]

Contrasts of Nature

Indeed, the Old Testament uses the term "son of man" in what are obviously pre-Christian contexts simply to assert the imperfect, creature qualities of the human species. In Numbers 23:19, for example, the expression specifically contrasts divine perfection with human frailty: "God is not a man, that he should lie, nor a *son of man,* that he should change his mind." Then there is the familiar question from David: "What is man that you are mindful of him, the *son of man* that you care for him?" (Ps. 8:4). Again, in similar words: "O LORD, what is man that you care for him, the *son of man* that you think of him? Man is like a breath; his days are like a fleeting shadow" (Ps. 144:3–4).

Most basically, therefore, to call anyone—including Jesus—a "son of man" is to acknowledge that he is beset by weakness, that he is subject to time and death. In his exalted and eternal status with the Father and Holy Spirit, Jesus was subject to none of the sorts of limitations we human beings know only too well. For the sake of what he wanted to do for us, though, Jesus voluntarily and temporarily subjected himself to everything that threatens humans. He did not cease to be divine, but he laid aside his divine prerogatives. Like a king who lays aside his crown and scepter in order to live among his subjects as one of them, Jesus retained his personal identity but forsook the privileges to which his identity entitled him.

Jesus was both God and man simultaneously during his incarnation. He neither desired nor sought to disguise either element of his total personality. Yet he would not coerce anyone to recognize or stand with him. Each person was left free to examine for himself, decide for himself, and declare for himself. Thus we go back to the critical discussion that took place in the coastal region of Caesarea Philippi about Jesus' identity. Who was he? What had the apostles been speculating about him? What had Peter decided?

Identified with Deity

Peter and the others would certainly have been able to discern his *deity* by being with him day after day. Indeed, what would *you* have said, if you had been in Peter's shoes on that day? His earlier teacher-mentor, John the Baptist, had pointed Jesus out to Peter as the one Yahweh had sent him to announce: "I have seen and I testify that this is the Son of God" (John 1:34). Peter had watched in amazement as Jesus had healed sick people (Matt. 4:23), made lepers whole with a touch (Matt. 8:1–4), and made blind people see again (Matt. 9:27–30).

He had even seen Jesus raise the dead! (Matt. 9:18–26). Add to these things the sermons he had heard from Jesus, the many private conversations in which Jesus had answered all his questions with uncanny insight, and the way Jesus responded to the accusing questions of his enemies. Then there was simply his goodness, his purity, his compassion! So Peter was ready and eager to confess that Jesus was God's Messiah. No, even more, he was ready and eager to acknowledge his sameness with God and therefore confessed him to be the Son of God.

Identified with Humanity

That was an all-important intuition and realization for Peter and his fellow-apostles. When he confessed him as the Son of God, Jesus was thrilled—and said so. "Blessed are you, Simon son of Jonah, for this was not revealed to you by man, but by my Father in heaven" (Matt. 16:17). Yet Jesus did not want Peter's excitement over seeing his deity to overwhelm and obscure another element of his identity that the apostle needed to grasp. It is as if Jesus felt compelled to say: "Peter, you've seen my *deity,* and that is wonderful! But look still more closely and see also my *humanity,* for that part of my nature is equally important for you to understand. If you do not understand that my identification with you in your weakness is complete, you may eventually be unable to grasp or believe that you can be united with me in glory—and thus might not be able to communicate it to others."

Suffered Rejection

Jesus would "suffer many things," including a rejection that would lead to his death. When Jesus told Peter this, the man who was overwhelmed with Christ's deity could not accept such a mortal fate for him. "'Never, Lord!' he said. 'This shall never happen to you!'" (Matt. 16:22). God doesn't suffer rejection. God doesn't suffer at all! And he certainly can't be killed! So Peter protested the absurdity that such a thing could even be said or contemplated—with reference to one whose sameness to God he had just confessed by calling him the Son of God.

Ah, but you have so much still to learn, Peter! There is so much more to Jesus than you can possibly grasp at this point in your emerging faith. You must be patient. In fact, Jesus told him, you are not even to try to tell people what you have come to see about Jesus yet—for your understanding is so incredibly incomplete at this point (see Matt. 16:20). As to Peter's outburst to Jesus that rejection and death would "never happen" to him, it almost takes away my breath to hear the rebuke: "Jesus turned and said to Peter, 'Get behind me, Satan! You are a stumbling block to me; you do not have in mind the things of God, but the things of men'" (Matt. 16:23).

Suffered Death

The language Jesus used sounds incredibly strong—even harsh—to us. But he had to be emphatic at this juncture in Peter's life. The fisherman-apostle wasn't ready to stand up with or to stand in for Jesus yet. He was still immature. He would still have his moments of doubt. He could still fold in a crisis. So it certainly wouldn't do to appoint him to the task of presenting, explaining, and defending Jesus yet. He still didn't know enough himself. And the primary thing he lacked at this point was the ability to appreciate that the Son of God could also be the Son of Man, that God could—and *would* by choice—suffer, die, and be raised. The path to Jesus' own glorification would pass through suffering and death. Peter wasn't ready for that and couldn't understand its necessity. Yet it was at the heart of Jesus' mission.

Confessed As Fully Man and Fully God

The significance of the truth that Jesus was "fully man" as well as "fully God" is what drove the church fathers to understand the phrase "Son of Man" to mean the humanity of the incarnate Son of God.

Heretics such as the Gnostics had claimed that Jesus was indeed truly God but that his humanity was only an apparent or make-believe humanity. In their heretical view, which exalted Greek philosophy over divine self-revelation, God could not take fleshly form, could not feel pain, could not experience death. Thus the things Peter and the other apostles affirmed about Jesus' death for our sakes could not actually be true events of space-time history. This "interpretation" of Jesus gutted the gospel message and left any who embraced it without a savior. Thus John would write: "Every spirit that acknowledges that Jesus Christ has come in the flesh is from God, but every spirit that does not acknowledge Jesus is not from God. This is the spirit of the antichrist, which you have heard is coming and even now is already in the world" (1 John 4:2–3). For John, the antichrist was not a still-to-come figure of the end times but a known reality. Anyone who cannot confess the full humanity—the Son of Man-ness—of Jesus has failed to appreciate the necessary truth of his complete identification with sinners that makes sinners' redemption through him possible.

CONTEMPORARY INTERPRETATION: MESSIANIC MAJESTY

Whereas the older interpretation of this title that traces back to the church fathers points to the humanity, weakness, and suffering of Jesus, the majority of modern scholarship sees it quite differently. Some even go so far as to claim that the interpretation of the church fathers "is in error" because of its failure to root the Son of Man motif more solidly in the Old Testament vision of Daniel.[4]

Indeed, there is a fascinating use of the term in Daniel 7. In the first year of Belshazzar's reign, the prophet Daniel had a disturbing vision that he described in these words: "In my vision at night I looked, and there before me was one like a son of man, coming with the clouds of heaven. He approached the Ancient of Days and was led into his presence. He was given authority, glory and sovereign power; all peoples, nations and men of every language worshiped him. His dominion is an everlasting dominion that will not pass away, and his kingdom is one that will never be destroyed" (Dan. 7:13–14).

Since no interpretation of this vision appears in the New Testament, we cannot be dogmatic as to its meaning. But a few things help us deal with this text as it relates to this title for Jesus.

For one thing, this vision is in the context of Daniel's dream about four beasts—a lion, a bear, a leopard, and a terrifying fourth beast that had tremendous destructive power. For another, most interpreters agree that the four beasts here parallel the four components—gold, silver, bronze, and iron mixed with clay—of an image Daniel had seen in chapter two. This leads many of us to conclude that the beasts represent, in turn, the four empires of Babylon, Medo-Persia, Greece, and Rome. If this much is correct, we at least have a time line for interpreting the scene.

As to the vision in question, the son of man in Daniel is obviously a human figure as opposed to another animal or beast. That he comes before the Ancient of Days, God Almighty, to receive "authority, glory and sovereign power" may suggest heaven's view of the event that left the apostles so bewildered, confused, and sad—Jesus' ascension to heaven following his resurrection.

As in Daniel's vision, that ascension took place in connection with heavenly clouds (Acts 1:9). And Jesus was borne from earth to heaven to be "exalted to the right hand of God" (Acts 2:33). True to the pattern of that vision, "Jesus thus follows the path of the Son of man up to the Ancient of Days and does not come down from heaven to earth."[5]

While again disclaiming dogmatism in view of the lack of a definitive New Testament interpretation of the passage, it is certainly possible for us to see Daniel 7:13–14 as a prophecy of the exaltation of God's Christ in the glorious resurrection and ascension of Jesus.

HOW SHALL WE UNDERSTAND IT?

How then should we interpret the title Son of Man in relation to Jesus? Shall we view it as the church fathers did and see it as a title of his humility? Or shall we embrace the more contemporary judgment that Son of Man is a title of majesty? I favor a both-and rather than either-or interpretation. Let me explain.

From Luke 9, we know that Jesus accepted the title Son of Man for himself. The same text also lets us know that he wanted Peter and the other apostles to understand the title in terms of the necessity of his suffering and death. Yet Daniel 7 clearly envisions the Son of Man as someone highly exalted by God and exercising an "everlasting dominion" that would surpass any human kingdom.

The New Testament invites us to see Jesus taking the unlikely path through suffering to exaltation. In his humility, he identified with us for the sake of our redemption. He became one with us in our weakness and modeled total dependence on the Father. His weakness led eventually to his death on a Roman cross. Yet God would not leave him in the throes of death. He brought him out of the dark tomb. In that act, Jesus "was declared with power to be the Son of God by his resurrection from the dead: Jesus Christ our Lord" (Rom. 1:4). Then, in his exaltation and coronation, the one who had already been shown to be Son of God, Christ, and Lord was additionally honored as Son of Man.

To the degree that we understand his identification with us, we also gain insight into the necessity of our identification with him. Our own "exaltation" must come through self-emptying and humility; our own "glorification" can come only through suffering with Christ. So James writes: "Humble yourselves before the Lord, and he will lift you up" (James 4:10). And Paul adds: "Now if we are children, then we are heirs—heirs of God and co-heirs with Christ, if indeed we share in his sufferings in order that we may also share in his glory" (Rom. 8:17).

WANGERIN'S "RAGMAN"

There is a story by Walter J. Wangerin that I would not know except that Phil Hasty shared it with me recently. Something I said in a sermon about Jesus' work of redemption triggered his memory of it. So he looked it up and faxed it to me. It has been on my desk ever since. Without repeating the story in all its details, let me summarize its essential point for you and tie the two themes in this Son of Man theme together with it.

In a city long ago, a ragman walked the streets and cried, "Rags! New rags for old! I take your tired rags! Rags!" He saw a woman sitting on her porch and sobbing into a handkerchief as her heart was obviously breaking. He walked up to her gently and said, "Give me your rag, and I'll give you another." The exchange made, he laid a clean linen cloth in her hand—so bright it forced her to shield her tender eyes. He took her old rag, started walking away, and then put the woman's handkerchief to his own eyes. He began to sob as pitifully as the woman had before. And she sat on her stoop without a tear.

"Rags! Rags! New rags for old!" came his cry again. Then he saw a little girl with empty eyes and a blood-soaked bandage on her head. Offering her a bright yellow bonnet for her ugly rag, another exchange was made. He put the bonnet on her head and tied her filthy bandage on his own. Incredibly, the wound seemed to go with the bandage. She was healed, but the Ragman began to pour blood from his head. Sobbing and bleeding now, he somehow managed to go on.

Wangerin's story continues as his narrator follows the trail of the Ragman. Next he came to a man leaning against a telephone pole. "Are you going to work?" the Ragman asked him. "Are you crazy?" sneered the man. With that, he pulled away from the pole and his jacket fell limp, for its sleeve was empty. He had no arm. "Give me your jacket," said the Ragman, "and I'll give you mine." He spoke with such quiet authority that the man did it. And the Ragman's healthy arm stayed in his jacket. When the crippled man put it on, he had two arms—strong and functional. But the Ragman now had only one.

Then the Ragman found a drunk lying under a blanket. He wrapped it around himself and left new, clean clothes in its place.

The little old Ragman—he came to a landfill. He came to the
garbage pits. And then I wanted to help him in what he did, but

I hung back, hiding. He climbed a hill. With tormented labor he cleared a little space on that hill. Then he sighed. He lay down. He pillowed his head on a handkerchief and a jacket. He covered his bones with an army blanket. And he died.

Oh, how I cried to witness that death! I slumped in a junked car and wailed and mourned as one who has no hope—because I had come to love the Ragman. Every other face had faded in the wonder of this man, and I cherished him; but he died. I sobbed myself to sleep.

I did not know—how could I know?—that I slept through Friday night and Saturday and its night too.

But then, on Sunday morning, I was wakened by a violence.

Light—pure, hard, demanding light—slammed against my sour face, and I blinked, and I looked, and I saw the last and the first wonder of all. There was the Ragman, folding the blanket most carefully, a scar on his forehead, but alive! And, besides that, healthy! There was no sign of sorrow nor of age, and all the rags that he had gathered shined for cleanliness.

Well, then I lowered my head and, trembling for all that I had seen, I myself walked up to the Ragman. I told him my name with shame, for I was a sorry figure next to him. Then I took off my clothes in that place, and I said to him with dear yearning in my voice: "Dress me."

He dressed me. My Lord, he put new rags on me, and I am a wonder beside him. The Ragman, the Ragman, the Christ![6]

Because Jesus so completely identified himself with us and our predicament, he was able to make atonement for our sins. As our single effective representative, he took the situation of sinful humanity onto himself and destroyed the power of Satan to hold us captive to it any longer. Now we can stand with him in solidarity as members of his spiritual body and in sure hope of sharing in his resurrection glory. He took our sin to himself and provided our justification; we receive his righteousness to ourselves and stand in his sinless perfection. "God put on him the wrong who never did anything wrong, so we could be put right with God" (2 Cor. 5:21, *The Message*).

As the Son of Man, Jesus modeled complete trust in and obedience to the Father (Heb 5:8). That example is for our instruction and imitation. In our natural and inherent humanity, we are called to live in dependence on God rather than self, in trust rather than disbelief, in obedience rather than defiance. Our inclinations all seem to take us in the opposite direction. We want to believe ourselves to be self-sufficient creatures and tend to chafe at the idea of bringing ourselves under the authority of parent, state, or God. So it often takes some life-altering calamity to slam us against the wall, impress us with our fragility, and set us on a search for what is real and permanent. And as we move in its direction, we meet the Son of God walking toward us as the Son of Man. Then he offers to exchange our rags for his clothing. The miracle of redemption occurs—and nothing is ever the same again!

CHAPTER FOURTEEN

JUDGE

of the Living and the Dead

ACTS 10:42

*He commanded us to preach to the people
and to testify that he is the one whom God
appointed as judge of the living and the dead.*

As PETER WAS EXPLAINING THE IMPORTANCE of knowing Jesus to his first Gentile acquaintance-student, he told Cornelius the basic facts of his life and work. Because the Roman soldier had attached himself to a Jewish synagogue as one of the "God-fearers" (Gentiles seeking a knowledge of Hebrew Scripture), Peter was able to tell the story against the backdrop of the Old Testament prophets.

> You know the message God sent to the people of Israel, telling the good news of peace through Jesus Christ, who is Lord of all. You know what has happened throughout Judea, beginning in Galilee after the baptism that John preached— how God anointed Jesus of Nazareth with the Holy Spirit and

power, and how he went around doing good and healing all who were under the power of the devil, because God was with him.

We are witnesses of everything he did in the country of the Jews and in Jerusalem. They killed him by hanging him on a tree, but God raised him from the dead on the third day and caused him to be seen. He was not seen by all the people, but by witnesses whom God had already chosen—by us who ate and drank with him after he rose from the dead. (Acts 10:36–41)

Here are all the essential facts about the Messiah/Christ and Lord, Son of God and Son of Man. Peter preached basically the same sermon as on Pentecost, adapted only slightly for his Gentile hearers: (1) Jesus fulfilled the predictions of Israel's prophets about the Messiah, (2) was authenticated to the public by the signs from the Holy Spirit, and (3) was ultimately declared to be Lord of all by his resurrection from the dead.

It is most interesting that Peter closed his lesson about Jesus by explaining the mission he and his fellow apostles were then carrying out: "He commanded us to preach to the people and to testify that he is the one whom God appointed as judge of the living and the dead. All the prophets testify about him that everyone who believes in him receives forgiveness of sins through his name" (Acts 10:42–43).

We have not finished telling the story of Jesus today until we declare him as Judge of the Living and the Dead and plead with people to believe in him for their salvation and hope.

VIEWS OF HISTORY

Perhaps the commonest view of history among ancient people was that it repeats itself endlessly and cyclically. Thus the Greeks and Romans, for example, paid little attention to past or future. They refused to study the past for its insights into why they were as they were; they had little interest in the future for the simple reason that they expected nothing truly new or unique to happen ahead of them. Our modern science of history writing certainly does not trace to these cultural forebears of ours.

The Epicurean View

Even for someone so brilliant as Plato, history was a boring repetition of confusing events, and salvation would come in being freed from our bodies and somehow merging into eternal, unchanging reality. The Epicurean philosophers of Paul's day summarized their view of history with these familiar words: "Eat and drink, for tomorrow we die!" In moments of spiritual depression, Solomon could wonder if life were not just that meaningless: "Generations come and generations go, but the earth remains forever" (Eccl. 1:4).

The Historical Progress View

After the huge acceptance of Darwin's theory of evolution over a century ago now, many modern historians adopted the view of historical progress that saw all things moving inevitably "onward and upward." Two world wars and numerous other glitches in the theory have caused most professional historians to modify—if not abandon—naive notions of inevitable advancement for the human species.

I have a hunch, however, that the historical-progress view of history has very deep roots in the general population. We seem to have put our hopes for the future in men and women who wear laboratory coats. We expect science to find ways to replace depleted resources on the planet, to cure all our diseases, and eventually to cheat death altogether. We will one day fix our environment, halt the aging process, and replace defective or worn body parts as we do now with lawn mower engines.

The Biblical View

The biblical view of history is another alternative of both the ancient and modern opinions just traced. The Bible's teleological (goal-in-mind)

165

view of human life says that God created the earth and populated it with males and females in his own image. He has revealed himself to us as the one God of power, truth, and love who is moving all things toward a grand consummation. Every human life is meaningful in view of God's purpose, and every human being may choose to participate with and be part of that purpose. When Jesus appears, he will bring all things to their finality and receive those who believe in him into eternal fellowship with God.

In the biblical view of history, all things are moving forward purposefully and deliberately. God has determined what I earlier referred to as the "grand consummation" and will achieve his prearranged goal. The target of all human history is the kingdom, the sovereign rule of God, and that predetermined purpose will not be defeated. Satan may attempt to thwart righteousness, and men and women may choose to defy God in their personal rebellion against the truth.

But evil and darkness cannot triumph over divine love and light! "The Bible throughout insists that God the Creator holds mankind eternally accountable for every thought, word and deed, and that each successive generation moves toward a final future in which the God not only of creation but also of redemption and judgment will consummate human history in the light of his divine offer of salvation."[1]

Jesus' Coming

The two most critical moments in the divine drama center on Jesus of Nazareth. The first was his appearance in the humble flesh and blood at Bethlehem; the second will be in triumphant glory when he comes at the end of time. The first coming brought Old Testament prophetic expectation to fulfillment and made the option of faith in him a defining reality for all of us; the Second Coming will bring New Testament prophetic expectation to fulfillment and begin the experience of everlasting joy for all who have accepted him as Savior, Lord, and Triumphal Lamb! Thus the earliest and commonest prayer of Christians has not been "Now I lay me down to sleep, I pray the Lord my soul to keep" or "God is great, God is good, let us thank him for our food" but *Marana tha*—"Come, O Lord!" (1 Cor. 16:22).

At his first coming, Jesus explicitly said, "I did not come to judge the world, but to save it" (John 12:47). True to his nature as the loving and compassionate Jesus, he would not bring things to conclusion without giving humanity its fullest possible awareness of the divine purposes at work. Anything that had not been made plain through a prophet-servant, he came to bring into the light. At his yet-awaited coming, however, circumstances will be different. There will be no time or need for additional revelation. The Second Coming will bring consummation, resolution, and triumph!

The thought of Jesus' return brings joy to the hearts of believers but surely must strike terror in the hearts of those who are living in rebellion against him. The plain facts of the matter are simply these: "[God] has set a day when he will judge the world with justice by the man he has appointed. He has given proof of this to all men by raising him from the dead" (Acts 17:31). The degree of confidence we have in looking toward that day is in direct proportion to our relationship with the Judge for that day.

THE CERTAINTY OF JUDGMENT

Consistent with a biblical view of history, God has repeatedly announced that his purposes are being unfolded in human events. He has revealed his will. He has overcome and punished those who have tried to defy his will; he has affirmed and blessed those who have participated in his purposes. In all this, he has taught humankind that we are accountable to him. But accountability is a fiction if there is no judgment.

Old Testament prophets spoke often of a coming "Day of the Lord." The Day of the Lord was a judgment in history—actually a series of judgments. First one nation and then another would be called to account for its treatment of Israel, Yahweh's covenant community (Joel 3:2;

see Amos 1:3–15). Indeed, even Israel itself would have its Day of the Lord and be called to account for its own deeds.

> But who can endure the day of his coming? Who can stand when he appears? For he will be like a refiner's fire or a launderer's soap. He will sit as a refiner and purifier of silver; he will purify the Levites and refine them like gold and silver. Then the LORD will have men who will bring offerings in righteousness, and the offerings of Judah and Jerusalem will be acceptable to the LORD, as in days gone by, as in former years.
>
> "So I will come near to you for judgment. I will be quick to testify against sorcerers, adulterers and perjurers, against those who defraud laborers of their wages, who oppress the widows and the fatherless, and deprive aliens of justice, but do not fear me," says the LORD Almighty. (Mal. 3:2–5)

Jesus and the apostles used the same motif of the Day of the Lord to point to the certainty of a final, ultimate day of reckoning in which every individual—among both the living and the dead—will be called into judgment. Consistent with Daniel's vision of "one like a son of man" to whom the Ancient of Days entrusted dominion and judgment, Jesus as the Son of Man announced his own role as Judge. Thus he questioned his disciples: "When the Son of Man comes, will he find faith on the earth?" (Luke 18:8; see Matt. 11:24; Mark 14:62).

Various New Testament writers picked up the theme of a final Judgment and affirmed it under the guidance of the Holy Spirit.

> For this very reason, Christ died and returned to life so that he might be the Lord of both the dead and the living. You, then, why do you judge your brother? Or why do you look down on your brother? For we will all stand before God's judgment seat. It is written:
> "'As surely as I live,' says the Lord,

168

'every knee will bow before me;
every tongue will confess to God.'"
So then, each of us will give an account of himself to God.
(Rom. 14:9–12)

Just as man is destined to die once, and after that to face
judgment, so Christ was sacrificed once to take away the sins
of many people; and he will appear a second time, not to bear
sin, but to bring salvation to those who are waiting for him.
(Heb. 9:27–28)

Harry lived in a cabin on the edge of Spirit Lake, just five miles from
Mount Saint Helens. When earthquake activity began under the mountain for the first time in 123 years on March 20, 1980, geologists warned
people to leave the area because an eruption was surely coming. Harry
ignored the warning. Then, on May 18, 1980, a magnitude 5.1 earthquake shook Mount Saint Helens. A major eruption of pumice and ash
poured out for more than nine hours. Fully thirteen hundred feet of the
mountain's peak collapsed or blew outward in the eruption. Millions of
tons of rock, ask, and mud rushed down the mountain at two hundred
miles per hour. Fifty-six people died, including Harry.

Harry didn't have to die, for he had ample warning of what was coming.
But there is something in us that says, "Maybe they're wrong" or "It won't
be as bad as they are saying." His decision to ignore or minimize the warnings led to his death. The decision of many to ignore or minimize the
warnings about death, judgment, and eternity will lead to their spiritual
deaths. No one will be brought to Judgment who has not been warned it
was coming. There will be no injustice on the part of the Judge on that day.

THE NATURE AND PURPOSE OF JUDGMENT

Most of the pictures of the Judgment we carry in our minds are likely
traceable more to some of the preaching we have heard than to the biblical

portrayal. Do you envision people stepping up one at a time to have courtroom-type trials? Do you see Satan prosecuting and hanging out all your dirty laundry with charge after charge? Does Jesus then reply to each charge to tell the Father whether it was committed before or after you were saved, and whether your repentance toward that deed is recorded? Will you be in suspense during a deliberation time, after which the verdict is announced? Frankly, I don't think the evidence from Scripture can be used to support such a television scenario.

Judgment before Jesus Christ in the last day is *not* for the purpose of determining guilt or innocence, condemnation or salvation. That issue has been settled already in a person's lifetime, and our fate is sealed at death. Do you remember, for example, the story of the rich man and Lazarus? Each had long ago made his choice as a Jew under the Law of Moses about living in harmony with God's kingdom purposes or in defiance of them. The one had lived as a pious man, though he had suffered from a terrible illness and had been treated with contempt by many who saw his horrible condition—including the rich man on whose property he had been known to beg.

The rich man had paid precious little attention to Moses and the prophets, and he had apparently been notable for his lack of compassion toward the poor and suffering. When they died, their eternal destinies were fixed, known, and entered. "The time came when the beggar died and the angels carried him to Abraham's side. The rich man also died and was buried. In hell, where he was in torment, he looked up and saw Abraham far away, with Lazarus by his side" (Luke 16:22–23).

With Jesus as Judge on that day, he knows those who are his own and confesses their names before the Father (Matt. 10:32). People of every generation, language, and race will come before him in two separate masses—sheep and goats, saved and lost, believers and unbelievers (Matt. 25:31–46). No surprises will occur at the Judgment about salvation. Those who have put their trust in Christ for salvation live and die in confidence; those who reject him for lesser things will learn once and for all what life has told them about the insufficiency of all but Jesus.

What, then, does the Bible mean by saying things like this? "We must all appear before the judgment seat of Christ, that each one may receive what is due him for the things done while in the body, whether good or bad" (2 Cor. 5:10). This text might be understood to mean that people's lives are going to be weighed in the scales of justice, with the good-to-bad ratio deciding our fate. But that would be inconsistent with every clear teaching of the New Testament about salvation.

Salvation is the result of a relationship with God through Jesus Christ, not the accumulation of enough good works to get us through the pearly gates. Since that is so, what *do* the passages about judgment based on our works mean?

Degrees of Reward and Punishment

The New Testament seems clearly to teach that there will be degrees of reward and punishment. Everyone who is saved is completely saved, mind you (Matt. 20:1–16). But is there no difference between the eternal state of a Christian martyr who suffered horribly for the Lord and someone like me? I've had it "easy" in my own spiritual life. I grew up in a Christian home. I had repeated encouragement to follow Christ. My adult life has had constant affirmations from Christians who love me. Where would be the *justice* in my having the same reward as one who kept faith with his or her Lord against repeated threats, torment, and death? At the least, would that person not have a far greater appreciation of the great reversal that will take place at Christ's coming when truth and righteousness are vindicated against their enemies?

Paul seems to point in this same direction at 1 Corinthians 3:10–23. Some Christian workers build with "gold, silver, costly stones" on the foundation, while others work with "wood, hay or straw." Each person's "work will be shown for what it is, because the Day will bring it to light." The work of some will survive; that of others will be burned up. "If it is burned up, he will suffer loss," says the apostle, "he himself will be saved, but only as one escaping through the flames."

This metaphor is not too difficult to understand. Think of someone who escapes a house fire but loses all her furniture, clothes, and personal items. She has been saved from the fire, but she escaped empty-handed. Is her rescue enough? Certainly. Is there still something unfortunate in her loss? Of course. All who are in Christ will be saved, but some will have misspent their energies on projects that bear no eternal fruit for him. In the Apocalypse, John writes: "Then I heard a voice from heaven say, 'Write: Blessed are the dead who die in the Lord from now on.' 'Yes,' says the Spirit, 'they will rest from their labor, for their deeds will follow them'" (Rev. 14:13).

Surely one of the most surprising things that will happen in that day will be the punishment of the wicked. Jesus' name is often used in obscene and profane ways in our culture. His cross has been made the object of shameful acts in modern "art" exhibitions. Worse still, his authority is defied. His willingness to save is rejected and scorned.

In this age, it appears that God is slow to act in the cause of justice. His apparent slowness calls into question God's power, his willingness to act, and even his existence. Evil, not God, appears to be sovereign. God's apparent impotence is manifested whenever the wicked prosper and the righteous suffer (see Ps. 73:1–16). Most tragic of all, the Righteous One suffered at the hands of the wicked. As an extension of Jesus' suffering, his followers suffer at the hand of God's enemies.

One day, however, we will witness a great reversal, as God acts to overturn this situation. Just as in raising Jesus from the dead God passed judgment in favor of his righteous Son, so also he will one day pass judgment on behalf of the righteous (Luke 18:1–8). This action will vindicate God as the one who in his good time does indeed bring to justice his enemies and those who persecute his people (2 Pet. 3:3–10).

Thereby, he demonstrated his wisdom and righteousness even to the cosmic powers (Eph. 3:10).[2]

Looking Forward to That Day

That Jesus Christ has been exalted to the right hand of God and will someday return as the Judge of the Living and the Dead fills my heart with confident hope. I know this world does not tell the full story of a human life. Believers will live into eternity with our Lord! So whatever happens in this life is to be kept in perspective for its temporary and limited effects. Let me list just a few of the areas of human life and experience where this matters to me.

Because Jesus Is Our Judge

I am not afraid that those who have died have perished or that death will harm me. Because Jesus is Judge of the Living and the Dead, I will not only see and be with my Heavenly Father reasonably soon but with my human dad and with saints whose stories have inspired me. I'll see that dear Christian lady who sent word for me to come see her in the hospital but died before I got there because I didn't know she was critically ill. As I have prayed with my friend Martha Alice over the past few weeks, we have been able to thank God together that her impending death is her path to healing that didn't come here. If I were to die today, grieve ever so slightly—then rejoice for me!

I can hold out hope to people who are living through hard times. Because Jesus is our Judge, he will bring about the great reversal that will vindicate the honest person working for a dishonest boss, the faithful spouse whose heart has been broken by betrayal, and the child who has been born with a tragic birth defect. Near the end of the first century, Christians were being persecuted. In a vision of those martyrs, John saw them under a heavenly altar and heard them crying, "How long, Sovereign Lord, holy and true, until you judge the inhabitants of the earth and avenge our blood?" (Rev. 6:10). Righteousness will have the last word, and those who have suffered most for Jesus' sake will receive the most beautiful crowns and most honored places near God's throne. No more than evil could keep Jesus in the darkness of the tomb can it defeat the holy and pure.

I know the Last Day will be filled with surprises. Yes, surprises, because Jesus is the Judge! We human beings judge things on the basis of our flawed values and impartial knowledge. Jesus will judge according to his perfect values and infinite knowledge—of both deeds and motives. He said, "There is nothing hidden that will not be disclosed, and nothing concealed that will not be known or brought out into the open" (Luke 8:17). Rather than hear this as a threatening passage, I hear it as a prophecy of surprises. We will find out that some of God's most effective and powerful saints were some of the quietest ones. We'll be shocked to know that we sat with them in church and never knew the burdens they bore with grace or the kindnesses they showed to people in distress (see Matt. 25:31–46). "Little" things we thought insignificant will be praised by our Lord as having eternal value. Many of the "least" will be declared "great," and vice versa. And we will be surprised.

I have a goal for every day that passes before his return. Because Jesus is my Judge, we can say: "Dear friends, now we are children of God, and what we will be has not yet been made known. But we know that when he appears, we shall be like him, for we shall see him as he is. Everyone who has this hope in him purifies himself, just as he is pure" (1 John 3:2–3).

Peter did not believe his preaching of the gospel to Cornelius was complete without telling him of the Day of Judgment. What a comfort it must have been for that Roman centurion to discover that the same person offering to save him would also be his Judge. Perhaps Peter used the same words Paul would later write to saints in the Imperial City to explain what that would mean for him: "Therefore, there is now no condemnation for those who are in Christ Jesus" (Rom. 8:1).

There is no reason for *you* to fear condemnation from Judge Jesus either. If you are in Christ today, you have the same right to assurance that Paul expressed: "Now there is in store for me the crown of righteousness, which the Lord, the righteous Judge, will award to me on that day—and not only to me, but also to all who have longed for his appearing" (2 Tim. 4:8).

Come, O Lord!

NOTES

Preface

1. The view of textual scholars is that Acts 8:37 is without merit for the original text of Acts of the Apostles. It is regarded as an insertion that reflects the practice of the early church. "Its insertion into the text seems to have been due to the feeling that Philip could not have baptized the Ethiopian without securing a confession of faith, which needed to be expressed in the narrative. Although the earliest known New Testament manuscript which contains the words dates from the sixth century (ms. E), the tradition of the Ethiopian's confession of faith in Christ was current as early as the latter part of the second century, for Irenaeus quotes part of it (*Against Heresies*, III.xii.8)." Bruce M. Metzger, *A Textual Commentary on the Greek New Testament* (New York: United Bible Societies, 1971), 360.

Chapter 1

1. The Editorial Committee of the United Bible Societies' Greek New Testament "was of the opinion that the original text of Matthew had the double name in both verses" but that the name Jesus was purposefully dropped from copies made of that Gospel due to "reverential considerations" for the name that quickly came to be regarded as uniquely belonging to Jesus of Nazareth by the early Christians. See Metzger, *A Textual Commentary on the Greek New Testament*, 67–68.

2. Colin Brown, ed., *The New International Dictionary of New Testament Theology*, vol. 2: *G-Pre* (Grand Rapids, Mich.: Zondervan Publishing, 1976), 332.

3. John 10:30; 14:10–11, 23; Matt. 11:27; Mark 9:37; see John 8:51–58; 20:26–29. Jesus' direct and indirect claims to deity in texts such as these will be explored in more detail in a later chapter dealing with the name-title "Son of God."

4. A typical house of that place and time would have looked very much like a box. The roof was flat, made of beams overlaid with a matting of small branches and mud-plaster. An outside stairway that allowed a family to catch the cooler evening air allowed the four men to carry their paralyzed friend onto the roof. Once there, they simply chipped and removed enough of the mud-plaster and branches to create an opening large enough to allow them to lower the man through the roof.

5. John Grisham, *The Street Lawyer* (New York: Doubleday, 1998), 126–127.

6. See 1 John 2:1–2. The reference in this text to "one who speaks to the Father in our defense" (NIV) or to "an advocate with the Father" (NRSV) draws from first-century court vocabulary and refers to a defense attorney. As our defense counsel, Jesus cannot plead our innocence. Instead, he confesses (with us) our sinfulness and offers (for us) his own body as the "atoning sacrifice for our sins."

Chapter 2

1. *The Zondervan Pictorial Encyclopedia of the Bible.* 1975 ed., s.v. "Immanuel, Emmanuel," by J. B. Scott III, 259.

2. John I. Durham, *Exodus* (Waco, Tex.: Word Books, 1987), 39.

3. Michael Card, *Immanuel* (Nashville, Tenn.: Thomas Nelson, 1990), 27.

4. Ibid., 28.

5. Desmond Tutu, *The Rainbow People of God* (New York: Doubleday, 1994), 55–56.

Chapter 3

1. "Fragment 41" in Philip Wheelwright, *Heraclitus* (Princeton: Princeton University Press, 1959), 102.

2. *Theaetetus* 202C and *The Sophist* 258B–C, 262E–263C.

3. *Metaphysics* 7p, 1012a, 23.

4. Leon Morris, *The Gospel According to John* (Grand Rapids, Mich.: Wm. B. Eerdmans, 1971), 120.

5. *Theological Dictionary of the New Testament,* 1967 ed., s.v., "*legō, logos, hrēma, laleō.*"

6. George Foot Moore, *Judaism in the First Centuries of the Christian Era,* vol. 1 (New York: Schocken Books, 1927), 416.

7. Philo, *Allegorical Interpretation* 3.96.

Chapter 4

1. James Montgomery Boice, *Foundations of the Christian Faith,* rev. ed. (Downers Grove, Ill.: InterVarsity Press, 1986), 314.

2. John 3:14; 6:51; 10:11; 11:49–57; 12:24; 18:11.

3. 1 John 1:7; 2:2; 4:9–21.

4. Revelation 5:6–14; 6; 7:9–17; 13:8; 14; 15:2–3; 19:7, 9; 21:9–27; 22:1, 3.

5. See John R. W. Stott, *Romans: God's Good News for the World* (Downers Grove, Ill.: InterVarsity Press, 1994), 115.

Chapter 5

1. G. B. Caird, *A Commentary on the Revelation of St. John the Divine* (New York: Harper and Row, 1966), 74–75.
2. Lloyd J. Ogilvie, *The Communicator's Commentary: Acts* (Waco, Tex.: Word Books, 1983), 92.

Chapter 6

1. See also Josephus, *Antiquities of the Jews*, 17. 10. 4, 8.
2. Matt. 21:9; Mark 11:9–10; Luke 19:38; John 12:13.
3. Acts 4:11; see Eph. 2:20–21; 1 Pet. 2:4–8.
4. Cited by Hoskyns and quoted in George R. Beasley-Murray, *John* (Waco, Tex.: Word Books, 1987), 169.
5. Leon Morris, *The Lord from Heaven*, 2nd ed. (Downers Grove, Ill.: InterVarsity Press, 1974), 98.
6. The summary of major points in Psalm 23 that follows is from John R. W. Stott, *Favorite Psalms* (Chicago: Moody Press, 1988), 32.
7. Stott, *Favorite Psalms*, 32.

Chapter 7

1. For other examples of hymns in the text of the New Testament, see Ephesians 5:14; Colossians 1:15–18; 2 Timothy 2:11–13; and Revelation 15:3–4; 22:7.
2. For helpful background and insights for this beautiful piece, see Ralph P. Martin, *The Epistle of Paul to the Philippians* (Grand Rapids: Wm. B. Eerdmans, 1959), 95–109.
3. *Theological Dictionary of the New Testament*, Vol. 3, 1965 ed., s.v. "*kyrios, kyria, kyriakos, kyriotēs, kyrieuō, katakyrieuō*" by Werner Foerster, 1039–1058. "One may sum up the whole development by saying that *kyrios*, originally the one who is fully authorized and has the legal power of disposal, did not contain the element of arbitrariness which so easily clung to *despotēs*" (1046).
4. *New International Dictionary of New Testament Theology*, 1975 ed., s.v. "Lord, Master" by H. Bietenhard, 512.
5. William L. Lane, *The Gospel According to Mark* (Grand Rapids: Wm. B. Eerdmans, 1974), 438.

6. *New International Dictionary of the New Testament*, 516.

7. In the section that builds off this material, the quoted block is taken from the original. The other comments mirror some of my own reflections prompted by the unfolding metaphor.

Chapter 8

1. Information on The Game of Life and The New Game of Human Life comes from William R. Mattox Jr., "In the game of life, immortality beats material gains," *USA Today*, 29 April 1998, 13A.

2. Ibid.

3. Bruce Milne, *The Message of John* (Downers Grove, Ill.: InterVarsity Press, 1993), 210.

4. Ibid., 211.

Chapter 9

1. Sally Quires, "We Have Suffered Too Long in Loneliness and in Fear," *Los Angeles Times*, 14 December 1997, A2.

2. William L. Lane, *Call to Commitment: Responding to the Message of Hebrews* (Nashville, Tenn.: Thomas Nelson, 1985), 80.

Chapter 10

1. D. A. Carson, "Matthew" in *The Expositor's Bible Commentary,* Vol. 8, ed. Frank E. Gaebelein (Grand Rapids, Mich.: Zondervan Publishing, 1984), 97.

2. Ibid.

3. Neil T. Anderson, *Victory over the Darkness* (Ventura, Calif.: Regal Books, 1990), 43.

Chapter 11

1. *The New International Dictionary of New Testament Theology*, Vol. 2, ed., s.v., "Jesus Christ, Nazarene, Christian" (Grand Rapids, Mich.: Zondervan, 1976), 336.

2. Morris, *The Lord from Heaven*, 29.

Chapter 12

1. "Father-son finish in '92 most eloquent," *USA Today*, 2 August 1996, 14E.
2. George Eldon Ladd, *A Theology of the New Testament* (Grand Rapids, Mich.: Wm. B. Eerdmans, 1974), 168–169.
3. *Monogenēs* is a compound word formed from *mono* (only) and *genos* (kind). It means one of a kind, singular, or unique. Plato uses it to refer to Earth in the cosmos, not the only planet but unique among them. It is also used in Hebrews 11:17 of Isaac; he was not Abraham's only (or only begotten) son but singularly and uniquely his son of promise. *Monogenēs* has nothing to do with begetting but with special status. Moulton and Milligan's *Vocabulary of the Greek New Testament* shows that "only begotten" would be *monogennētos* rather than *monogenēs*.
4. *Berakoth* 40a; *Sanhedrin* 70b.
5. Joachim Jeremias, *New Testament Theology* (New York: Charles Scribner's Sons, 1971), 67.

Chapter 13

1. One could claim that John 12:34 is an exception to this rule. In this instance, however, Jesus' hearers are only echoing his words and asking him to make clear for them the identity and nature of the Son of Man.
2. Tutu, *The Rainbow People of God*, 28–29.
3. C. S. Lewis, *Mere Christianity* (New York: The Macmillan Company, 1952), 154.
4. Ladd, *A Theology of the New Testament*, 146.
5. *The New International Dictionary of New Testament Theology*, s.v. "Son, Son of God, Son of Man, Servant of God, Son of David," by Otto Michel as revised and updated by I. Howard Marshall.
6. Walter J. Wangerin, *Ragman and Other Cries of Faith* (San Francisco: Harper and Row, 1984).

Chapter 14

1. Carl F. H. Henry, *God, Revelation and Authority*, Vol. 2: *God Who Speaks and Shows* (Waco, Tex.: Word Books, 1976), 312.
2. Stanley J. Grenz, *Theology for the Community of God* (Nashville, Tenn.: Broadman and Holman, 1994), 823–824.